4-23-05

To Vie
Best Wishes

[signature]

BUCKETS
OF MONEY

BUCKETS OF MONEY

How to Retire in Comfort and Safety

Raymond J. Lucia, CFP®

with Dale Fetherling

WILEY

John Wiley & Sons, Inc.

Published by John Wiley & Sons, Inc., Hoboken, New Jersey
Published simultaneously in Canada

For general information on our other products and services, or technical
support, please contact our Customer Care Department within the United
States at 800-762-2974, outside the United States at 317-572-3993 or fax
317-572-4002.

Wiley also publishes its books in a variety of electronic formats. Some
content that appears in print may not be available in electronic books.

ISBN: 0-471-47866-0

Printed in the United States of America

10 9 8 7 6 5 4 3 2

Dedication

To my wife Jeanne, my best friend and soul mate for over 30 years. She is a pillar of strength who has patiently stood by me, tolerating my crazy schedule of radio, television, client work, and study. Thank you for allowing me the time to write this book and pursue my passion.

To my children—Alana, Ray Jr., Dom, and Niki—who have been the joy of my life and a great inspiration. I couldn't be more proud.

To my mom and dad, who not only fed me well (a little *too* well, actually) but gave me a true sense of values and taught me that family, not money, is the most important thing.

To my brother Michael Lucia, ChFC, a terrific financial advisor whose dedication and work with clients has helped and motivated me immensely.

To my staff of financial and personal advisors—including Melissa Dotson, Rick Plum, CFP®, Rob Butterfield, JD, Marc Seward, ChFC, and the rest of my team with whom I work and learn from each day.

And to the almost 4,000 clients who are using the *Buckets of Money* strategy. They have entrusted me and my firm with their money, a responsibility we take very seriously. It is because of them and people just like them that I have written this book.

A Special Note

When I began writing this book, we were well into the middle of the greatest boom in stock market history. Talking about conservative investments for immediate income and reasonably conservative money for "tomorrow," along with a modest allocation to equities and real estate, wasn't very popular. Everyone was making big bucks on their individual stock bets, high-tech mutual funds, dot-com IPOs, day trading, and the like.

But by mid-March 2000, a brutal bear market was born. Who would have thought that many stalwart companies like Cisco Systems, Sun Microsystems, Oracle, and even Home Depot, Microsoft, Disney, and General Electric would lose up to 80 percent of their value? Then, on September 11, 2001, the country was shocked and appalled when terrorists attacked America by flying hijacked jetliners into the World Trade Center towers in New York and into the Pentagon in Washington, D.C. This further roiled the financial markets.

Anyone invested in the stock market since March 2000 has been hurt financially by the bursting of the tech bubble, which then was compounded by this terrorist tragedy. But despite the short-term impact on the stock market and the toll such events take on consumer confidence, the U.S. economy is still quite resilient, and stocks will one day return to become respectable investments. Because no one can forecast tragedy or its effect on the financial markets, it is even more critical that individuals have their *Buckets of Money* set up properly.

We know that time, for the most part, mitigates risk, and *Buckets* will help you do that. But while neither *Buckets of Money* nor a soaring bull market could ever cause us to forget those who innocently lost their lives on that tragic day, the events of the last couple of years do help us to understand the importance of planning. I hope this book will motivate you to do just that.

—R.J.L.

Note on Tax Rates

Reduced tax rates are a centerpiece of the federal Jobs and Growth Tax Relief Reconciliation Act of 2003. But the recent tax law, like the one enacted in 2001, is a patchwork of provisions that phase in and out in sporadic fashion. So here's something you can take to the bank: The tax code will change again before long. That presents a problem for this book because some tax-rate figures could be obsolete by the time you read them.

For example, the tax on long-term capital gains and dividends has been lowered to 15 percent for higher-bracket taxpayers. But those cuts are now scheduled to expire in 2009. Similarly, the 5 percent long-term capital gains/dividend rate remains in effect for lower-bracket taxpayers (10 percent or 15 percent ordinary-income bracket), then drops to zero for 2008. These reduced rates expire after 2008 and are scheduled to revert to previous levels in 2009. Whether that will happen—or be changed again—is anybody's guess.

So, in the interest of sanity and clarity, we have stuck with the 2003 brackets—generally 35 percent, 33 percent, 28 percent, 25 percent, 15 percent, and 10 percent—as well as the 15 percent capital gains/dividend rates in our examples. If the tax laws are changed again or if these rates are allowed to expire, you may choose to mentally adjust the rates mentioned in the examples.

Contents

Part IV *Bucketizing* Your Life

Part V Living Happily Ever After As a *Bucketeer*

Preface

What *Buckets* Can Mean for You

O.K., right off the bat, here's a pop quiz (but it's an easy one). Are you:

	Yes	No
■ Retired?	___	___
■ Thinking about retiring?	___	___
■ Starting to worry about whether you'll have enough money to retire?	___	___
■ Managing your own money?	___	___
■ Disturbed by the stock market's sometimes violent swings?	___	___
■ Concerned about inflation eating away at the purchasing power of the money you worked so long and hard for?	___	___

If you answered "Yes" to any of those questions, you can profit from the *Buckets of Money* strategy. In short, it's a way of *generating steady income while still taking advantage of the historically proven growth in stocks and other long-term investments.*

That's not doublespeak: Achieving both goals—income and growth—is not only doable, it's a smart and conservative way to protect *and* grow your nest egg. In fact, in almost 30 years as a financial planner who oversees nearly a billion dollars in assets, I have found nothing as simple—and as powerful—as this concept.

But first, let me be clear about what *Buckets of Money* is *not.* It's not a get-rich-quick scheme. It won't make you as fabulously wealthy as you would be if you had invested big time in Microsoft 25 years ago. (You missed that opportunity, huh? So did I.) *Buckets of Money* doesn't involve some high-wire act like futures trading, currency arbitrage, penny stocks, or dealing in distressed real estate. You don't have to predict the future, and you won't need to raise chinchillas, plant jojobas, or be atop the crest of some so-called technological wave of the future.

All you need to do is know your financial goals, divvy up your money accordingly, and then invest intelligently, according to guidelines I'm going to give you in this book. It's a conservative—but growth-oriented—strategy that hopefully will allow you to:

- Live comfortably in retirement without having to work (though you may choose to)
- Sleep well at night without worrying about your money running out

Let me hasten to add, *Buckets of Money* is not a plan without risk—*no* investment is ever totally risk-free. How the overall economy fares, the way the financial markets perform, and the ups and downs of your particular investments will affect the results you get. We do not predict any specific outcome. Having said that, let me tell you that this is a sound way to reduce risk while still taking advantage of growth. What's more, I know hundreds, perhaps thousands, of people, probably very much like you, who have used the *Buckets of Money* principle to build and enjoy a financially comfortable retirement.

Sad to say, I've also seen many people begin their retirement thinking they had enough money to live on for the rest of their lives. But the twin dangers—inflation and taxes—ate away at their financial cushion until they either had to cut back drastically on their standard of living or go back to work just to survive. Sometimes they depleted their estates so much that the legacy they hoped to leave for their children was but a fraction of what they intended. Please, *don't* let that happen to you.

Speaking Bluntly

To put it bluntly, the object of financial planning for retirement is to avoid running out of money before you run out of time. The focus of the *Buckets of Money* strategy is taking advantage of the long-term potential of stocks and other equity-type investments while securing a safe, predictable income from assets. It's especially appropriate for retirees and those looking to enhance income while reducing risk. However, the *Buckets* principle works for everyone, regardless of age, income, net worth, or investment experience.

In brief, here's how it operates: You put your money into three "buckets" and invest each in a different way. (As you become a more informed *Bucketeer*, you'll find that from time to time you may need more than three buckets because some will hold pretax money, some post-tax cash, etc. But for the sake of simplicity, let's just talk for now about the three main buckets.) The cash deposited in Bucket No. 1 goes into very stable, low-growth vehicles like CDs, money markets, Treasury instruments, and short-term bonds. Using both principal and interest, Bucket No. 1

provides a stable income stream that you can live off for a specified number of years. (Don't panic at the thought of spending both principal and interest. You'll see later why we totally deplete Bucket No. 1.)

Meanwhile, your Bucket No. 2 is growing. This bucket, depending on your tolerance for risk, may be invested in slightly more aggressive investments with better potential for returns. After Bucket No. 1 is empty, you pour money from Bucket No. 2 into Bucket No. 1 for yet another specified period of years.

By the time Bucket No. 1 is again depleted, Bucket No. 3—full of stocks, real estate, and similar high-growth investments—will have had all that time to grow, and with any kind of luck at all you'll then have a nice chunk of change to see you through your sunset years. Although Bucket No. 3 is more risky, that risk is mitigated by time. So if Buckets Nos. 1 and 2 last 12 to 14 years, that should provide an ample cushion in the event the stock market takes a short-term dive requiring a few months or even a few years to recover. Also, as you'll learn later, an allocation to low-leveraged real estate investments may provide an extra cushion during a prolonged bear market for stocks.

That's the short course. Naturally, there are lots of variations, such as how much you put in each bucket, how long you let it grow, and the kinds of investments that are right for each bucket. We'll go into all that, as well as how to make sure that you're covered for emergencies that may pop up.

Among the big advantages of *Buckets* is its simplicity. Even a rookie investor can understand and make use of the basic philosophy. Another advantage is that *Buckets* is flexible enough for the more sophisticated investor, that person who likes to get every last one-quarter of a percentage point of return and who seemingly follows the financial markets with a magnifying glass. Further, you can modify your *Buckets* program as your situation changes. If you get a windfall, you need more cash to live on, or you want to increase or decrease your potential return and your exposure to risk, the strategy is easy to alter.

So, relax and enjoy this book. I've tried to make it as simple and clear as possible. Believing that an ounce of application is worth a ton of abstraction, I've used plenty of examples and have sought to avoid financial gobbledegook.

As you learn about this strategy, think about your goals and how you might adapt the *Buckets* program for your situation. Keep in mind, too, that there are no perfect solutions, no absolute answers, and no right and wrong ways to invest. Each person's investment objective, comfort level, risk tolerance, and tax situation will determine the best investment choices to fill each bucket.

What Do I Know?

Having been a financial planner since 1974, I've seen good times and bad. For over 12 years I've also fielded thousands of money questions on my nationally syndicated radio talk show (details, see www.raylucia.com) and responded to a flood of e-mails and letters. I've studied the financial markets and have seen interest rates at 18 percent and 3 percent and everywhere in between. I have watched the real estate roller coaster create moguls and paupers. I've seen quick-buck artists come and go (sometimes to jail). I've seen salesmen so slick they could sell a stethoscope to a tree surgeon, yet didn't have the slightest idea of what they were talking about.

I've seen it all, and this is what I've learned: You've got to analyze your particular situation because that situation is unique to you. Therefore, be cautious about taking advice you see in the magazines or on TV or hear discussed on the radio or at your weekly bridge game. The advice may be true for some but totally inappropriate for you. Once you've analyzed your situation, then you've got to allocate your assets in a way that's smart and sound. This takes patience and some wisdom, too.

The wisdom part, which I'll discuss in the last chapter, means knowing that money, as important as it is, is not the object of the game. Playing a good game is the object of the game. Speaking of games, I once heard someone describe a perfect football player: smart enough to understand the plays and dumb enough to think they're important. I'd propose a variation of that for the perfect investor: smart enough to know how money works but not dumb enough to think that's only what life is all about.

What does money represent in your life? A necessary means to an end, or an end in itself? Hold that thought. We'll get back to that.

How This Book Works

A few words are in order about how this book is organized. The first two chapters give the big picture on handling your money long term. In essence, because nobody is smart enough to predict what will happen to the economy next year or even five years from now, an intelligent asset-allocation program is your best bet for being able to meet rising costs without worry.

After exploring your tolerance for risk and explaining the *Buckets* principle in more detail in Chapters 3 and 4, Chapters 5 through 7 tell how to choose the best investments for each bucket and also go into some of the tax issues. The next two chapters suggest how to tweak the buckets in special situations, regardless of the kind of retirement savings—401(k), Keogh, IRA, Roth IRA, CDs, etc.—that you may have.

If the recent bear market knocked a 'hole' in your *Buckets* plan, Chapter 10 gives some damage-control pointers. Chapter 12 tells how to find a financial planner and what other steps to take to put your finances on a sound path. Lastly, Chapter 14 includes a bit of wit and wisdom. In the Appendices, you'll find a list of other books and resources I think you might enjoy and profit from.

This book will teach you the basics of *Bucket* planning and *Bucket* filling. If you carefully follow the strategies discussed you will become a master *Bucketeer*, and, I truly hope, live a financially fulfilling life!

A Product of Many Hands

This book is a product of many hands. My sincere thanks go to all who contributed to it, especially Rob Butterfield, Jr., Esq.; Rick Plum, CFP®; Michael Lucia, ChFC; Marc Seward, ChFC; Melissa Dotson; Ray Lucia, Jr., CPA; Lyn Rowe, CFP®; Janean Stripe, CFP®; John Dean; Bill Izor, CFP®, CLU, ChFC; Ryan Bowers, CFP®; Susan Bowers, CFP®; Mike Sztrom; LuAnn Porter; and Dale Fetherling.

PART I

INTRODUCING THE *BUCKETS*

CHAPTER 1

Everybody's Got an Investment Idea— But Is It a *Good* Idea?

If there's anything we've got plenty of in our Information Age, it's advice about how to make a bundle. Money gurus promise wealth without risk. Financial magazines trumpet the latest trends. The Internet virtually bristles with offers. Our neighbors or co-workers eagerly share their astounding stock market secrets. The daily mail overflows with wealth-building tips.

As a result, many of us are surrounded by opportunities, flooded with information—*much of it wrong*—and are often totally confused about how to build a nest egg so we can enjoy a decent retirement. Actually, what most people want to know is simply:

- How can I retire in reasonable comfort?
- How can I know my retirement funds will keep pace with inflation and taxes?

- How can I protect myself from the short-term swings in the stock and bond markets?

Those are increasingly urgent questions for an astounding number of people. Here's a startling statistic: The number of Americans 65 and older will grow almost five times faster over the next 40 years than those in the 20-to-64 age group. What that means is that tens of millions of workers—far more than in any other era in our history—will soon reach the end of their working lives. So "How can I retire successfully?" is a question that's quickly moving to the top of the agenda for many of us.

The answer needn't be complicated. But like all things worth doing, becoming investment savvy requires some study and some perseverance. I'm going to try to cut through the fog. I'm going to talk straight about why and how you should be thinking about your money and your future.

I'm not out to prove I'm smarter than you are or that I have all the answers. In fact, I know I don't have all the answers, and I may not be smarter. But I'm smart enough to know you shouldn't need a fancy financial vocabulary or a degree in finance to do some common-sense planning for your future.

My Bias

Right up front, here's my bias: *I like facts.* I like proven principles, not just accepted wisdom or broad generalizations. I agree with Oliver Wendell Holmes, who once said, "I never heard a generalization worth a damn, including this one." So I'm going to emphasize what is provable and scientific and show you the fallacy of so much of what is generally believed. I'm going to tell you, based on more than a quarter-century of helping people with their money, what really works and what doesn't. Further, I'm going to promulgate *Lucia's Laws*—many of which may be the direct opposite of the investment axioms you've heard for years. And with any kind of luck, you will not only learn some things but also have a few grins along the way.

Why All the Concern about Retirement, Anyway?

Americans are living longer, a lot longer. A century ago, life expectancy was 47.3 years. Now it's 76.5 years on average, and in a few decades it will be 82.6. Millions upon millions—quite possibly you among them—will live to be more than 100. (The future Willard Scotts will be very, very busy.) In fact, already the number of people 65 or older has grown by 56 percent since the 1970s. For the first time in history, there are more seniors than teenagers!

Meanwhile, workers are retiring earlier, voluntarily or otherwise. Although your parents and grandparents may have died on the job or within a few years after retiring, many of your generation will live 20, 25, or 30 years after quitting work. All this is good news for those of us in our middle or later years, right? Sure—*if* you plan for it. But consider:

- There's enormous uncertainty about life spans. One study showed that even if you toss out extreme cases—where both spouses died quickly or lived to be very old—among those who remain, the second spouse to die might live to be 83 or last to age 97. If you're in that big middle group, you may need to fund an 18-year retirement, *or* one that lasts 32 years. That's an enormous range.
- Seventy percent of all couples 65 or older will have one or the other spouse in a nursing home. The average stay in a nursing home is 2.7 years at approximately $52,000 a year, or about

$140,000, almost none of which is covered by Medicare. And the costs are accelerating at a rate that far exceeds inflation.

■ Despite these demographics, the median savings among adults in their late fifties—just the age when we start thinking seriously about retirement—are less than $10,000.

Even if you're lucky enough to stay out of a nursing home and avoid a big nonreimbursable medical expense, living longer is likely to erode your resources as inflation eats up more and more of your savings. Although you may plan to leave money to your kids or favorite charity, you might end up needing every penny saved—and then some.

I'm not trying to scare you with these statistics. But I am trying to make you aware that the reality of retirement is that—unless you plan ahead and act on those plans—you can very easily run out of money before you run out of years. And that's not so good. It's not good for you, for your children, or for society. And what's more, it's in many cases a preventable problem. That's what this book is all about: helping you become self-sufficient in retirement. Which leads us to . . .

LUCIA'S LAW 1

The government isn't going to take care of you.

I'm sorry. I wish it were otherwise. But even if its much-discussed problem of too many beneficiaries being supported by too few workers is fixed, Social Security just isn't going to be enough. Social Security was intended to be a financial side dish, not the main course. Don't assume you're going to be pleased with what's on your plate if Uncle Sam is the only cook you're counting on.

Meanwhile, the number of active workers covered by company pensions is fast declining. The reasons are numerous. Employees now are less likely to stay at one firm for a long time. Pension plans are costly to run. Pensions at some firms have taken a back seat to stock options and other benefits. Thus . . .

LUCIA'S LAW 2

Don't count on your employer to take care of you, either.

Company pensions are being dismantled in favor of plans like the 401(k), the 403(b), Simple IRAs, and others that shift the burden of saving and investing from employers to employees. These plans can be confusing. But they also give the retiree lots of opportunities.

So the bad news is that it's up to you to make plans. But the good news is that for most people, that's doable. With a bit of smarts and some time, we ought to be able to do this. And we *can.*

The Twin Demons—Inflation and Taxes

In addition to greater longevity, inflation and taxes are two other factors to keep in mind as you begin to think about your retirement nest egg. You're probably old enough to remember the late 1970s and early 1980s—leisure suits, *Mork and Mindy,* and double-digit inflation. Rates on CDs (certificates of deposit) got up to 15 percent or more. A great time to be an investor, right? *Wrong.* Returns after taxes and inflation often were in negative territory, meaning that although you received higher interest payments, your purchasing power—your "real" rate of return—actually declined. (Figuring your real rate of return is easy. Take the yield on your fixed investment, subtract the percentage you'll pay in taxes, and then subtract the rate of inflation.) When interest rates were 15 percent, inflation was also in double digits. And the real rate of return on fixed investments was under water.

Compared to then, inflation right now is relatively tame. Still, inflation is always present and over time will rob you. Even with inflation at 3 percent, the purchasing power of a dollar is cut in half in a little more than 23 years. That means in two decades you'll need twice as much money to buy what you do now.

Similarly, taxes can take away much of what you make. So we need to think about tax-managing our money. One example I often use in my seminars illustrates the effect of such taxes. Let's say Christopher Columbus, when he sailed across the ocean blue in 1492, put $1 in a savings and loan and let it earn interest. What do you think that'd be worth today?

Well, 500 years is a long time (longer than *my* investment horizon). But at simple interest, Chris would now have amassed only $26—that's $25 in simple interest, plus his original invest-ment of one buck. Aha, you say, what if the interest were com-pounded? If the interest was compounded but earnings were taxed annually, Columbus would now have $6.9 million. Interest on interest is a *beautiful* thing!

But here's the kicker: If the interest was compounded but the taxes were deferred, the good captain would now have $39 *bil-lion*, with a "*B.*" So you see just how important compounding in a tax-controlled environment can be. Keep that in mind. We'll come back to that.

And Your Point Is ... ?

My point is that in any investment strategy you choose, you not only want to make your money grow, you also need to take infla-tion and taxes into account. Which leads to . . .

It's not what you make . . . but what you
keep *that counts.*

It's that "real" rate of return that will be so important. By real rate, I mean your after-tax, after-inflation rate of return.

What You've Heard about Stocks Is True, Sort of

For years now you've probably heard that the stock market is the place to be. Its growth averages more than 10 percent a year. Can any CD or money market fund match that? No, it can't. With savings accounts paying 2 percent or 3 percent, stocks look pretty good. Yes, indeed.

Further, you've doubtless heard that some people—maybe those you know at work or on the golf course—hit it big with Qualcomm, AmericaOnline, or Somethingorother.dot-com—and made an incredible bundle. Possible? Yes.

In fact, I believe I can safely say . . .

If you don't invest in stocks,
you won't be financially prepared for retirement.

Figure 1.1 shows the return from stocks, bonds, and cash before and after inflation. Stocks, as you can see, have a decided edge in terms of real return. So if that's the case, why not just put your money in the stock market, sit back in your chaise lounge, and

Figure 1.1

reflect on your soon-to-be luxury yacht and million-dollar villa? Well, it's not that simple, and Figure 1.2 shows why.

Figure 1.2 is my EKG. No, just joking! Actually Figure 1.2 shows the *wide* fluctuations in the Standard & Poor's (S&P) 500 index over the years (. . . but my EKG probably does look like that during periods of market turbulence). The stock market is a real roller coaster because, for starters, there are some 20,000 stocks, and they're not all winners—and even the winners don't win year in, year out. And the overall market doesn't perform consistently. That 10 percent-plus average growth figure you've heard about is just that—an *average*. It may be up 30 percent one year and down 20 percent the next. (Be wary of averages. The average American family, for example, consists of 2.6 persons—but how many have you seen like that?)

No doubt about it, stocks are risky—at least in the short term. In fact, stockbrokers and mutual fund managers are so fond of one phrase that they put it in almost all their literature: "Past performance is not necessarily an indicator of future results." That means, "We don't have any idea what's going to happen." And it's true, they don't. *No one* does.

So that unpredictability is a problem for those who are trying to plan for retirement. Because what do you want when you retire? You want to be able to count on a certain level of income, right? Sure. You also want that income to grow to cover inflation. If stocks and the equity markets are the places to be, but stock prices bounce every which way, how are you going to get that kind of certainty? Good question. I'm glad you asked that. Because that's what this book is all about.

However, before we get into the details of the *Buckets of Money* principle, let's look at why the usual methods of investing in the stock market don't work. You may recognize some of these money-making methods, maybe even some that you're so fond of that you use them yourself. But keep an open mind, and I predict

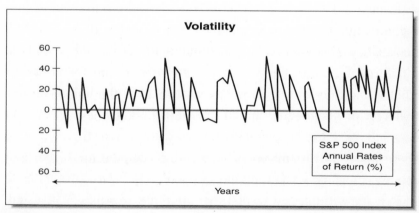

Figure 1.2

that as you see the shortcomings of these other efforts, the logic of *Buckets of Money* will become clear.

Ideas That Sound Good—but Aren't Good and Sound

Time the Market

Yes, the market jumps around a lot. We all know this. So what do we do? Well, if we can anticipate those jumps and sell just before it goes down and buy just before it goes up, we'll be golden, right? Yes, we would be golden, indeed.

But here's the rub: *Nobody is smart enough to do that.* The market is affected by all sorts of factors, here and abroad: interest rates, government policies, consumer confidence, bad news, good news, currency fluctuations, the ups and downs of earnings, and even the health of heads of state. Not me, not you, not Warren Buffett, not Bill Gates, not Peter Lynch knows what's going to happen tomorrow or even five years from tomorrow.

In fact, speaking of Lynch, I once interviewed him. I asked this fabled money manager at Fidelity Investments what he thought was ahead for the stock market. "We'll see," he said. I asked him the same question about the bond market. "We'll see," he repeated. I asked him about interest rates, and he said, "If I could predict the direction of interest rates three times in a row, I'd be a billionaire." This was Peter Lynch, the most successful and admired money manager of his generation and one of my heroes, and he doesn't know. If *he* doesn't, neither do you or I.

In about 20 of the last 70 calendar years, stocks have lost money. In truth, when the market makes big gains, it often does so in leaps within a few days' time. So if you're not fully invested, it's easy to miss a major move.

In short, you can't predict a good day. As Figure 1.3 shows, $1 invested in the S&P 500 for 20 years (1982–2002) would have grown to $10.94. But miss just the 16 best months (out of 240) in that 20 years, and you end up with only $2.79. The moral is that *It's better to stay invested in a broad array of good stocks or good mutual funds.* But most people don't. They get impatient. They see that some other fund or stock is going gangbusters, and they can't help but chase the front runners. They get a hold of that 1-800-SWITCHMYFUND number and use it all the time to jump on this fund or drop that one—and end up shooting their portfolio in the foot. As you probably have figured out by now, I'm not the biggest fan of market timing.

That's because it *can't* be done. I'm certain of it, and many studies bear this out. And if timing really worked, everybody in the know would do it. Then it would be a self-defeating exercise

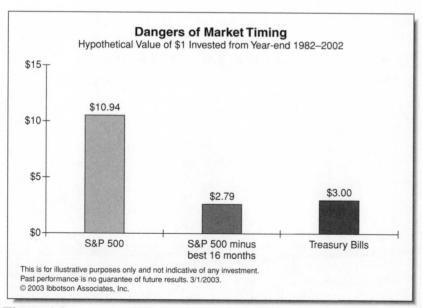

Dangers of Market Timing
Hypothetical Value of $1 Invested from Year-end 1982–2002

This is for illustrative purposes only and not indicative of any investment.
Past performance is no guarantee of future results. 3/1/2003.
© 2003 Ibbotson Associates, Inc.

Figure 1.3

anyway. The truth is, stock prices move—up or down—so rapidly and sometimes so utterly without warning than even if you were able to get out of the market before it took a tumble, you wouldn't know when to get back in. Thus, you'd likely end up worse off than if you'd never gotten out.

Which is exactly what happens to market timers and which bring us to . . .

LUCIA'S LAW 5

Too much trading can be hazardous to your wealth.

As I say, you can't predict a good day. And if you pick a bad day to get in or out of the market, you may be paying for it for a long time. Figure 1.4 shows the results of a five-year study in which the more investors traded, the less well they did.

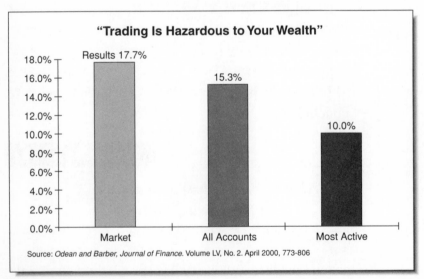

Figure 1.4

Follow the Leader

Another tactic that leads investors astray is following the latest financial Pied Piper. Millions of people scan the ratings of mutual fund managers, for example, to find those whose funds performed best the previous year. But rarely is "Past performance is not necessarily an indicator of future results" more true than here.

After all, whom would you choose: the manager who made the most money in the 1987 crash, or the one who lost more than average in 1987? Well, according to the *Hulbert Financial Digest,* in the five years following the 1987 crash, the managers who did best in the crash made 1.4 percent while the crash losers earned an average of 5.1 percent. (Why are we even buying all these magazines that purport to tell us who the best fund managers are? Beats me. Maybe we should be looking for lists of the *worst* managers!)

In fact, *Hulbert* reports, for the decade ending in 1992, if you jumped each year to the best fund manager of the past 12 months, you'd have gained 51.2 percent over 10 years. But if you had begun each year investing with the *worst* manager of the previous 12 months, your account would have gone up 220 percent over the same period! Even so, both would have earned less than the S&P 500 Index, which climbed 308 percent during that time.

Thus, I conclude . . .

LUCIA'S LAW 6

Trying to pick the best mutual fund
is an exercise in futility.

A whole financial magazine industry has sprouted up around the idea of trying to get you into the hottest of the 10,000 or so mutual funds. But, according to one study, the reality is this: If you pick a manager or a fund that finished in the bottom fourth of all funds, you have a 50 percent chance of finishing above the median five years later. And if you pick a top-quartile manager or fund, you have a 48 percent chance of finishing above that same median. So, in short, it seems to me that whether you pick the top fund or the worst, your chances of doing well over time are about the same.

The predictive abilities of the magazines and newsletters don't amount to much over the long term. Even the much-vaunted Morningstar ratings service, while great for the information it provides, hasn't been flawless when predicting future winners. Don't get me wrong—I believe Morningstar has tremendous resources, and I use those resources every day. But Morningstar, you, and I are not clairvoyant. All fund ratings are based on what happened yesterday, but no one knows what will happen tomorrow. My advice: Pick what seems to be a mix of good but diverse funds and stick with them.

As for those self-proclaimed investment gurus who flood you with junk mail or claim on TV to have a lock on future riches, they're doing little more than reading tea leaves. Ask yourself: If their strategy is *so* great, wouldn't they be so really, really rich that they wouldn't need to appear on infomercials selling some get-rich-quick scheme? You bet.

Be American, Buy Only American

Another strategy people bandy about is to stay away from foreign stocks. Overseas companies are less safe, these investors say. I say, "Nuts to that." Yes, our economy has often done well in recent decades. But don't make the mistake of believing that the international markets have nothing to offer. Figure 1.5 shows that

Figure 1.5

while the American stock market did well over the past 32 years, it wasn't the best-performing market.

Two decades ago, as author Ric Edelman points outs in *The Truth About Money*, America accounted for almost 50 percent of the world's total stock market capitalization. Today, it represents 43 percent. Does that mean we're in decline? Actually, it just means that we're a smaller piece of a very rapidly growing pie. And that's why you need to have at least some of your money in international stocks.

While I usually recommend an allocation of 10 percent to 20 percent, Figure 1.6 shows how you can put as much as 40 percent of your portfolio in foreign equities and have no more risk—and a *much* higher potential return—than if you were totally invested

Figure 1.6

in U.S. stocks. Thus, if you don't invest overseas, you may miss out on the often stellar performance of international stocks.

Stick with One Investing Style

Others advocate using just one style of investing. Value investors, for example, look for bargain stocks that have been beaten down and are due for a rise; they buy low in hopes of later selling high. Growth investors, on the other hand, like more expensive, high-flying companies; they buy high in hopes of selling even higher. Still others prefer to concentrate on certain sectors, such as only large companies, or only small companies, or just those in the energy field or the retail field or the electronics field . . . or *something*. But none of those schemes work consistently.

And just because you're invested in a mutual fund rather than an individual stock doesn't mean you're diversified. Some stock funds are so specialized that they are almost as risky as owning a single firm's stock. (What's more, even a stock fund's name can be misleading. The manager of a large growth fund may load up on small-capitalization stocks when they're hot. It pays to read the prospectus and annual report.)

The truth is, all styles of investing are cyclical and fraught with peril. Figure 1.7, for example, shows how the results of investing by styles defy predictability. Figure 1.8 illustrates how the return of different investment classes varies markedly from year to year.

Figure 1.7

Relative Performance of Market Sectors

1985	1986	1987	1988	1989	1990	1991	1992	1993	1994	1995	1996	1997	1998	1999	2000
FOREIGN STOCK	FOREIGN STOCK	FOREIGN STOCK	SMALL CAP Value	LARGE CAP Growth	BONDS	SMALL CAP Growth	SMALL CAP Value	FOREIGN STOCK	FOREIGN STOCK	LARGE CAP Growth	LARGE CAP Growth	LARGE CAP Growth	LARGE CAP Growth	SMALL CAP Growth	SMALL CAP Value
LARGE CAP Growth	LARGE CAP VALUE	LARGE CAP Growth	FOREIGN STOCK	LARGE CAP VALUE	LARGE CAP Growth	SMALL CAP Growth	LARGE CAP VALUE	SMALL CAP Value	LARGE CAP Growth	LARGE CAP VALUE	LARGE CAP VALUE	SMALL CAP Value	FOREIGN STOCK	LARGE CAP Growth	BONDS
SMALL CAP Value	BONDS	LARGE CAP VALUE	LARGE CAP VALUE	SMALL CAP Growth	LARGE CAP VALUE	LARGE CAP Growth	SMALL CAP Growth	LARGE CAP Growth	LARGE CAP VALUE	SMALL CAP Growth	SMALL CAP Value	LARGE CAP VALUE	LARGE CAP VALUE	FOREIGN STOCK	LARGE CAP VALUE
SMALL CAP Growth	LARGE CAP Growth	BONDS	SMALL CAP Growth	BONDS	SMALL CAP Growth	LARGE CAP VALUE	BONDS	SMALL CAP Growth	SMALL CAP Value	SMALL CAP Value	SMALL CAP Growth	SMALL CAP Growth	BONDS	LARGE CAP VALUE	SMALL CAP Growth
LARGE CAP VALUE	SMALL CAP Value	SMALL CAP Value	LARGE CAP Growth	SMALL CAP Value	SMALL CAP Value	BONDS	LARGE CAP Growth	BONDS	SMALL CAP Growth	BONDS	FOREIGN STOCK	BONDS	SMALL CAP Growth	BONDS	FOREIGN STOCK
BONDS	SMALL CAP Growth	SMALL CAP Growth	BONDS	FOREIGN STOCK	FOREIGN STOCK	FOREIGN STOCK	FOREIGN STOCK	LARGE CAP Growth	BONDS	FOREIGN STOCK	BONDS	FOREIGN STOCK	SMALL CAP Value	SMALL CAP Value	LARGE CAP Growth

Figure 1.8

The Moral of the Story

Just as we've seen all along, nobody is smart enough to know what's going to be in favor or out of favor in five years or so. Still, folks make wrong, short-term decisions all the time and for the wrong reasons. They buy high when a stock or mutual fund is said to be "hot." And then they sell in a panic when, inevitably, it dips.

Ric Edelman puts it so succinctly: "Stocks are not the problem—you are the problem, because you let your emotions get in the way."

Edelman and I and every other capable financial planner say you must invest in stocks if you're going to keep ahead of inflation. But by now you're probably asking: "If, as you say, I need to be in the market but I can't begin to time its ups and downs, and can't consistently pick the best stocks or funds, and can't count on the best managers, and can't rely on a certain style of investing, how can I financially prepare for retirement?"

The answer: Buy quality, well-diversified investments, and then have a plan that gives you the means as well as the discipline and/or courage to hold them for years. That's also—*surprise!*— the gist of the *Buckets of Money* principle. But before we jump right into *Buckets*, let's look more closely at the important question of what we mean by "diversified."

CHAPTER **2**

Why Your Grandmother Was Right After All!

A lot of folks, perhaps you among them, hate the idea of financial risk. To these investors, the wild plunges and peaks of the stock market seem to epitomize such risk taking. They feel they worked hard for that money, they and/or their kids are going to need it, and by gosh, they don't want to fritter it away by investing it in something that's as likely to go down as it is up.

That's understandable. But it's also short-sighted and self-defeating.

Every investment involves risk. Truth is, even *not* investing involves risk. (Hoarding cash under your mattress may give you a sense of security but it doesn't protect you if the house burns down or, much more likely, if inflation devours the purchasing power of those greenbacks.) So understand . . .

LUCIA'S LAW 7

There's nothing wrong with putting your money at risk.
In fact, it's impossible not to.

So the real question isn't, Shall I risk my money? You will, no matter what you do. The real questions are, *How* shall I risk my money? *How* can I get some measure of protection while taking a small, calculated risk? In short, although every investment includes risks, wisdom consists of knowing what the risks are and which ones are worth taking.

Let me give you an example that financial planners sometimes use of how risk can help you. Let's say you have $50,000 to invest for 20 years. If you chose a 4 percent CD, your account would grow (before taxes) to $110,000. You would have risked little, except for the effect of two decades' worth of inflation.

But just for the sake of argument, imagine instead that you divided your $50,000 evenly as follows:

- $10,000 in an old coffee can buried in your backyard. At the end of the two decades, you'd still have a soggy $10,000 in an old coffee can.
- $10,000 as an interest-free loan to your less-than-reliable Uncle Charley. As you feared, he fails to pay you back, so at the end of the 20 years, you'd have zip, zero, nothing from him.
- $10,000 in a bank account earning 2.5 percent interest, giving you $16,385 at the end of the period.
- $10,000 in a Treasury bond earning 5.5 percent. In 20 years, you'd have $29,175.

- $10,000 in the stock market, where it earns the historical average of 11 percent over the 20 years, amounting to $80,620.

So, you earned nothing on the first chunk. You essentially threw away the second amount by giving it to your deadbeat uncle. You got minimal returns on the low-risk bank account and a modest return on the super-safe government bonds. Only that last $10,000 had much upside potential. Yet, adding this all up, your total return is $136,180—far more than you would have earned by stashing the whole amount in the ultra-safe CD.

How can that be? How could you throw away $10,000, earn nothing on another $10,000 and next to nothing on a third increment, and still far outpace the CD returns? *Because you took a little more risk.* Not a lot more—remember: Just one-fifth of your savings went into stocks. But that was enough to boost your returns handsomely.

Also keep in mind that you can't lose more than the amount you invest. Thus, the $10,000 that you effectively threw away is still $10,000. But the amount you can make with a stock investment is, in return for some risk, potentially unlimited.

The trick, then, is to diversify your investments in such a way as to minimize your chances of losing everything and maximizing your shot at some big bucks. Or as my sainted Italian grandmother used to say, "Nontchu putta alla u eggsa inna wona basaket," which translated means, "Don't put all your eggs in one basket." Granny, though a little lacking in the details, had the right idea.

You don't want to take foolish risks; you don't want to be rash. But you need to be willing to take *some* risks to have any hope of a decent return. If you're one of those people who try to insulate themselves from risk by sticking only with low-risk, low-return investments, you're guaranteeing failure. Or to put it another way . . .

The biggest risk may be taking too little risk.

What Is Risk?

Keener minds than mine have long struggled with how to quantify risk. The best gauge they have come up with is something called *standard deviation*. I don't want to get too technical here about how it's figured. What's important at this point is only that you know what it means. So consider this: An investment's rate of return bounces around—or "deviates"—each year. If it bounced around the same amount each year, this deviation would become "standard." But, of course, it doesn't. So deviation measures the amount of annual fluctuation (and thus, the risk) that an investment can be expected to have. The higher the standard deviation, the greater the expected fluctuation and the greater the risk.

An investor who knows the standard deviation is much better armed than if he merely knows the average return (because an investment's return is almost always higher or lower than its average). So when I talk about risk or when you see charts in this book that compare risks, the yardstick that's being used is standard deviation. Again, the higher the standard deviation, the greater the volatility and the greater the risk.

For example, Figure 2.1 shows the return and risk of three different portfolios. The one at the bottom (35 percent government bonds, 50 percent stocks, and 15 percent cash) has no more risk than the 100 percent government-bond portfolio but has a far better return. Naturally, you want low risk and high return, so that's the superior portfolio of the three.

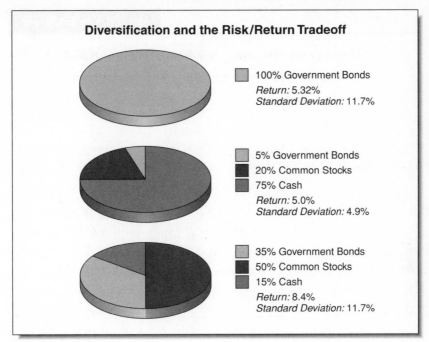

Figure 2.1

We can experiment with different combinations to come up with different degrees of risk and return. Figure 2.2, for example, shows the risk versus return of several kinds of investments over a long period. Notice that the Treasury bills are low-risk, low-return investments. But as you move to the right (toward more risk), the returns start going up. It's that diversification—putting your money in more than one kind of investment—that gives portfolios the best shot at optimal returns.

How do we achieve diversity? Through what's called *asset allocation*. Asset allocation, in brief, means that what's important is not which stocks you buy but what proportion of your assets you have in the stock market as opposed to other investment categories. Or, to quote me again (I'm *so* articulate!) . . .

Forget about picking the next Home Depot or Fidelity Magellan. Instead, get the right asset mix.

This isn't just my brilliant idea. It's based on research that led to the 1990 Nobel Prize in Economics. A very smart guy named Harry Markowitz came up with the foundation of diversification when he looked at what's the best way to make money in the stock market. (I enjoyed a delightful lunch with Mr. Markowitz one day, but I must admit to a strong case of "brain overload" as

Figure 2.2

I attempted to keep up with his incredible mind. Afterward, I figuratively kicked myself for not studying harder in my college statistics courses.)

Not All Risks Are Created Equal

In effect, Markowitz developed techniques to help achieve the maximum likely overall return with the least possible risk. Such methods, called *modern portfolio theory*, are now routinely used by sophisticated investors and pension plan trustees. The basic idea is that the total risk of a portfolio depends not just on the risks of an individual investment, but also on the correlation between those risks.

As I've said before, all investments entail risk. But not all entail the *same* risk. Bond prices, for example, are very sensitive to interest-rate changes. Stocks are, too, but less so than bonds. CDs, fixed annuities, and guaranteed investment contracts fluctuate even less. Thus, in a period when interest rates are going up, you'd have less risk with a portfolio of bonds *and* stocks and CDs than you would with a 100 percent bond portfolio. Make sense?

You can build a portfolio that's safer and more profitable by investing in many asset classes (for example, stocks, bonds, real estate, cash) than you can by investing in only one class. It might seem paradoxical, but introducing an element of stock market risk (for example, going for a 20/80 stocks/bonds mix instead of 100 percent bonds) can actually reduce the overall risk over time.

In fact, studies have shown that more than 90 percent of the variability of a portfolio's return is based on asset mix, not on what individual stocks you choose, how well you time the market, or how lucky you are. To effectively diversify, you might divide your portfolio into numerous classes, say, large-company stocks, small-company stocks, international stocks, fixed-income investments, guaranteed investment contracts, and real estate.

Tailoring for Your Tolerance

You can—perhaps with help from a financial planner—further tailor these stocks, funds, and other investments to match your risk tolerance. That means deciding between growth or value in the large- and small-cap stock sectors, between emerging and developed nations in the international sector, and between long-term or short-term and high credit or lower credit ratings in the fixed-income sectors. Then, regularly adjust your portfolio to keep the asset allocation balanced over time.

Although he hardly needs my ratification of his ideas, Markowitz was *right.* Such a portfolio provides better returns at a lower level of risk and volatility. Having a properly diversified portfolio means your returns probably will never be at the top of the pack. But they won't be at the bottom, either.

Why is that? Because most people don't have just one or two stocks; that would be way too risky. Instead, they own a bunch of stocks or funds, and their results aren't going to be too terribly different from the broad stock market averages. If you owned just a few companies, you might wallop the averages—*or* get walloped. But as you add more stocks to your portfolio and add bonds, real estate, and cash to your overall investment mix, you lower both your odds of greatly outpacing the market *or* of suffering a major beating if and when stocks head south. And that's very important because once you've lost money, it's tougher to get back to where you were. For example, as Figure 2.3 shows, if your $100,000 nest egg drops by 25 percent, you need a *33 percent* gain to get you back to the original amount.

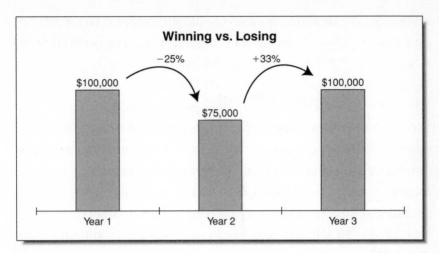

Figure 2.3

Investing to minimize loss must be part of any investment strategy. Thus, I humbly suggest . . .

LUCIA'S LAW 10

The best way to win is to keep from losing.

It's like that example I talked about earlier in this chapter, the one where you threw away a sizable chunk of your investment but still recouped by having a portion in stocks. You didn't earn as much as if you had put the whole $50,000 into stocks. But, still, you did well—and *without the risk* that you'd have faced if you had been totally invested in stocks and there was a market collapse.

Diversification can help with your *real* rate of return, too. That's because not all investments are taxed the same or react similarly during inflation. For example, bonds produce interest and stocks generate dividends. Under current law, taxable bond interest payments are subject to ordinary income rates, and stock dividends are taxed at capital gains rates. That gives the distinct advantage to stocks from a tax standpoint because if they are held for more than a year, both dividends and the gain are taxed at a maximum rate of 15 percent. Thus, bonds, although far less risky, are not nearly as tax-efficient unless you buy tax-free municipal bonds. More on tax management later.

Some asset classes (such as stocks and real estate) tend to do better in inflationary times than do fixed-income and cash investments. During periods of economic difficulty, bonds excel as interest rates decline. So, again, diversification—and a financial planner—can help you here. Figures 2.4 and 2.5 show the effect of taxes and inflation on different kinds of assets.

Figure 2.4

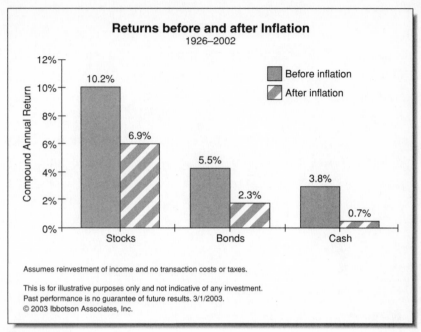

Figure 2.5

The Joys of Rebalancing

Notice that I said it's not enough just to diversify, you must also rebalance from time to time. That means setting targets for what percentages of your money should be in various assets (say, 60 percent in stocks, 20 percent in bonds, and 20 percent in cash), then readjusting your portfolio from time to time to bring it back in line with these targets. For example, Figure 2.6 shows how a stock and bond mixture can get out of whack because stocks generally grow more quickly than bonds, and Figure 2.7 shows how a portfolio might be tweaked to bring assets back into balance. If the portfolio isn't rebalanced, the stocks eventually would take up more and more of your portfolio, increasing your exposure to risk if there was a steep stock market downturn.

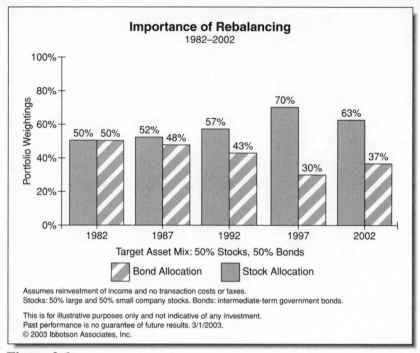

Figure 2.6

Imagine a 70/30 mix of stocks and bonds, as shown in Figure 2.6, being rebalanced back to the prescribed 50/50 mix. Instead of having 70 percent of your money exposed to the grizzly bear market that hit stocks with a 50 percent decline starting in March of 2000, only half the portfolio would have suffered the decline while the other half in bonds would have gained significantly.

Your family may have taught you about this concept of rebalancing. I know mine has. That's because when I go to Las Vegas and get on a winning streak, my tendency is to double down and bet the farm on a hot hand. My wife Jeanne, bless her heart, has been known to scoop up some chips when I'm not looking and stick them in her purse. If I flame out, we still can go home with some winnings, thanks to her, because she has reduced our risk.

Rebalancing your portfolio is much the same. Rebalancing among stocks, bonds, real estate, and cash keeps your portfolio's risk level under control. In addition, rebalancing *within* a stock portfolio (for example: adjusting to a level of 50 percent blue-chip, 25 percent small-cap, and 25 percent international stocks) also could reduce risk if an overweighted sector suffers a setback.

Rebalancing also could mean taking some dough out of other assets and putting it into stocks if they are beaten down to bargain prices. For example, bonds have been on a tear in the recent past while stocks have been mostly in the doldrums. Reallocating some money to stocks from bonds, or vice versa, may prove to be

Figure 2.7

profitable over the long term. In 2003 the yield on the 10-year Treasury dropped to about 3.1 percent, culminating what may have been an end to a lengthy bull market in fixed-income investments. Yet many investors were caught off guard as interest rates jumped more than 1 percent in a six-week period, causing losses in what are typically the safest investments—government bonds. The point is, you readjust your investment portfolio to keep in sync with your goals and your prescribed asset allocation.

This can be fairly simple and painless in a tax-deferred retirement account, such as a 401(k). But if your stocks are in a taxable account and/or if you pay commissions when you buy and sell, rebalancing can be costly and involve messy tax accounting. One way to avoid those problems is to direct new investment dollars to those investments that have become underweighted. If stocks and bonds are outstripping your cash, for example, divert the money that you'd normally add to stocks and bonds into cash equivalents. Or you could take the dividends, interest, and mutual fund distributions that are produced by your stocks and bonds and add them to your cash allocation.

To get your model back to its original proportions may seem to you like selling some of your winners and buying your losers—and that's what it is. But that may be a very good thing to do. If you don't rebalance, eventually you'll own almost all stocks and will have abandoned the concept of diversification.

It's not good to abandon diversification—just ask any tech-heavy investor who made a bundle in 1996–1999, but gave most of his winnings back in the "tech wreck" of 2000–2001 and beyond. Rebalancing would have taken a few chips off the table, locking in at least some of those gains in companies like Cisco, Sun, Juniper, and JDS Uniphase before they tumbled.

Of course, you may not want to go back precisely to your original model. Your marital status, health, income, and other circumstances could have changed and, thus, your model may be altered.

How often should you reallocate or rebalance? Some people do it every couple years. Others do it when, for example, one asset class varies by some percentage from its initial weighting. I say: Whatever works for you is fine. In truth, *when* you do it is not as important as *making a commitment to doing it.*

So, Just How Risky Is the Market?

Ask me if the stock market is risky, and I'll ask you *how long* you expect to invest in it. Figure 2.8 shows the reduction in risk over time in small-company and large-company stocks, government

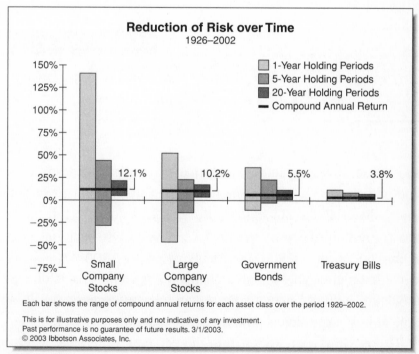

Figure 2.8

bonds, and Treasury bills. Notice how the volatility shrinks with time. The longer you are invested in stocks, the less likely you are to have a loss (or for that matter, a phenomenal gain). Studies show that you've got about a 1-in-4 risk of losing money if you invest in stocks for one year. That's an important principle: Risk declines sharply the longer you remain in the market. And it's yet further evidence that you win by not losing. Please remember:

LUCIA'S LAW 11

The only antidote for stock market risk is time.

And a corollary . . .

LUCIA'S LAW 12

If you have less than a five-year time horizon in the stock market, you're a gambler, not an investor.

In a sense, investing in the stock market is primarily about time and only secondarily about money. When stocks fall, it's tempting to dwell on the money lost. But that loss doesn't really matter if you don't need to sell. In fact, if you're building up your retirement accounts, you'd probably prefer the market's gains to come later, after you've had a chance to build a big portfolio. A downturn now can actually be a plus for you because you'll be able to buy more shares with the same amount of money.

If you view your stocks from the perspective of time, you're more likely to make smart decisions and less likely to be unnerved when the market dives. If you're patient, well-diversi-fied, and have a long enough time horizon, you'll probably do okay. But if you own just a few stocks or are heavily invested in a single sector, your wait could be awfully long for the market to spring back after a plunge.

Lessons Learned?

I hope I've shown you that being totally risk-averse is, well, *risky*. And, further, I hope I've convinced you that:

- Although the stock market does fluctuate and often wildly so, you're more likely to meet your retirement goals if you own stocks as well as real estate, bonds, and cash over the long term.
- What stocks and mutual funds you choose is much less impor-tant than the proportion of your portfolio they occupy.
- You've got to take a long-term view to allow the stock market trend to work for you.

And that, my friends, is a guiding principle of the *Buckets of Money* strategy: buying time to let the stocks and other long-term investments grow—while having enough income to live com-fortably while that happens.

PART II

UNDERSTANDING

THE

BUCKETS

CHAPTER 3

What Kind of Investor Are You?

Meet the Nelsons, Ned and Nellie. Nice, hard-working folks, they are very proud of the fact that they have accumulated $300,000 in investable assets over their working years. The Nelsons want to enjoy their retirement, of course, and being conservative, they also want to make sure they don't lose any of that 300 grand. They toiled long and hard and did without in order to build that nest egg, and they wouldn't feel comfortable risking their principal by investing in the stock market or making some other iffy investment.

What's more, they hope to leave most of that sum to their children and their grandchildren some day. So for the Nelsons, caution is the order of the day. Call them the Nervous Nelsons.

So what do they do? They keep the $300,000 in the bank, mostly in certificates of deposit. For them, it's perfect: The bank *guarantees* them an income on the money *with no risk to their principal.* And the deposit itself is insured by an agency of the government. What a deal!

At an assumed rate of 6 percent interest (a bit high by today's standards but okay for our example), the Nelsons will earn $18,000 a year. That's not an enormous amount but the Nelsons are frugal, and with their Social Security added in, they'll get by. Equally important for them, they will sleep well at night. The FDIC backs the CDs up to $100,000 and with multiple accounts, all $300,000 could be insured. So they will still have their $300,000 no matter what. They've achieved, the Nelsons believe, safety *and* comfort. But *have* they? No. *No,* in a very big way.

If inflation averages just 3 percent a year, the purchasing power of their yearly $18,000 in interest will almost be cut in half in two decades. That means buying the same amount of groceries, gasoline, and everything else will cost nearly twice as much. It also means that as prices rise, the Nelsons will probably need to cash in some of their CDs just to get by. So their $300,000 is almost certain to shrink as they are forced into using more and more of it for everyday expenses.

Even if they somehow managed to keep the $300,000 intact, its *real* value—the amount it could purchase—will be closer to $150,000 than $300,000 after 20 years. And that's not at all what they had pictured and not what they intended to leave to their heirs.

Now the Nervous Nelsons really should be nervous. They chose such a conservative path that it could potentially lead them to go broke slowly. Or, as I like to put it . . .

LUCIA'S LAW 13

Safety without performance doesn't equal very much.

Above all, the Nelsons wanted their money to be safe. But they paid a big price for that illusion. They discovered a paradox: Focusing just on safety is a very *unsafe* way to invest. In fact, doing so practically ensures that you will fail financially.

CDs—sometimes called "certificates of *depreciation*" by financial wags—are not the basket you want to put all your eggs in. Yet CDs—and their close cousins, government or municipal bonds—remain the investment of choice for many retirees like the Nelsons who prefer the apparent stability of CDs and bonds and the solidity that somehow attaches to something purchased from a bank or the government.

Banks, particularly for a lot of seniors, have an aura of respectability. That image wins banks a lot of business. And that's fine. I'm in favor of respectability and in favor of banks—they do a good job at what they're designed to do, which is facilitate transactions. Banks are the perfect place in which to place your paycheck or Social Security benefit and then write checks on those accounts to pay your bills. They're also a good place to safely keep some cash while it's waiting for its ultimate destination. But as a place to store your retirement cache, no way! As I like to put it . . .

LUCIA'S LAW 14

Leaving a lot of dollars in the bank is like leaving a bunch of hamburgers on the grill. They'll shrink right before your eyes.

Banks as well as credit unions and savings and loans keep your money for you and pay you some interest to help keep abreast of inflation. So do Treasuries and government bonds. But where's the *growth?* Not in banks, not in savings accounts or CDs, not in government bonds. And you've got to get growth if you're going to build those retirement savings so they can support you through what may be a long retirement.

Safe from What?

Back to the Nelsons. They kept their money in a bank CD because it was supposed to be safe. But was it? And safe from *what?* Well, it was safe in the very narrow sense that there is a government-sponsored insurance system designed to prevent a loss to depositors if the bank should default—that is, go out of business. (If default protection is your primary goal, investing in government securities would be even safer.) And it's safe in the sense that the Nelsons will get back their principal (but not the same purchasing power).

But while it's mildly reassuring that the bank probably won't go under and take the Nelsons' money with it, inflation and taxes pose much bigger risks to Ned and Nellie. And their CDs don't help them much there. Even if the inflation rate is 3 percent, that's half the interest rate of their hypothetical CDs. So half of what they earn in interest is eaten up by inflation. Further, those interest payments are taxed at the Nelsons' regular income tax rate. As a result, the Nelsons would probably be lucky to break even—and may even lose money from their safe investment.

In fact, the Nelsons' investment strategy is causing their savings to dwindle. They won't feel the loss immediately, but eventually they'll find their money is virtually all gone, if indeed their income keeps pace with inflation. Which may be a lot like having the dentist pull your tooth *slowly.*

On the other hand, take the Hendersons, Harry and Sherry. Harry read somewhere that the stock market has averaged something in excess of 10 percent per year returns since 1926. Harry, who considers himself shrewd, knew that CDs didn't pay anything like that. Neither did corporate bonds or Treasury securities.

So Harry and Sherry decided to go for it and invest all of their $300,000 in the stock market. They enjoyed doing the calculations: They should have $330,000 by the end of the first year, $363,000 by the second, $399,300 by the third year, and so on. In a little more than seven years, they figured, they would have doubled their money! They would have more than $600,000 in their retirement kitty—and then let the party begin! Call them the High-Rolling Hendersons.

It is true that if the market produced *annual* gains of 10 percent, the Hendersons could easily draw down an inflation-indexed $18,000 per year and still leave a ton of money to their kids after they die. But, unfortunately, Harry and Sherry didn't read far enough, or maybe they chose to ignore the obvious. That 10 percent figure was an *average* gain, not one that occurred year in and year out. In fact, in some years, the stock market went down, *way down.* And sometimes way down for several years in a row.

A serious lesson in investing began, for example, in March of 2000—the beginning of the "tech wreck." From that point the broad market indices lost about 50 percent, and tech stocks dropped almost 80 percent from their highs. Similarly, in 1973–1974, the market also fell by almost 50 percent. And after that drop, it took almost 13 years for an investment in the broad market to have earned enough to equal the guaranteed rates of CDs or Treasury bills.

If the High-Rolling Hendersons had retired and invested their $300,000 in a market like 1973–1974, and then like the Nervous Nelsons, had taken out $18,000 each year to live on starting the year after a 50 percent decline, they would have been flat broke in just 17 years, even if the market averaged 10 percent annually for each year thereafter.

The Hendersons got greedy. By putting all their eggs in the stock market basket, they were attempting to get rich quick. But by trying to do so they opened themselves up to enormous risk, proving the wisdom of what I'll now call . . .

LUCIA'S LAW 15

Try to get rich quickly—and you may
get poor even quicker.

Yes, the stock market eventually came back from the 1973–1974 debacle (and, it's hoped, we'll see a recovery from the grizzly bear of 2000). But it would have been too late for the Hendersons. It turned out they had neither comfort nor safety.

So, you see, both the Nelsons and the Hendersons went broke. The risk-averse Nelsons went broke more slowly, but nonetheless just as broke because inflation ate away at what they thought was theirs forever. They were saddled onto an old horse called *safety,* and they rode it even as it collapsed and died on them.

By contrast, the Hendersons hitched themselves to what they thought was a shooting star that would arch endlessly across the financial sky. But we all know what happens to meteors—eventually, they crash or burn.

Using vastly different investment strategies, both the Nelsons and the Hendersons failed miserably at securing a safe, comfortable retirement. You can do better than they did, a lot better. To do so, you'll want to achieve a degree of safety (like the Nervous Nelsons) *and* you'll want growth (like the High-Rolling

Hendersons). But not one to the exclusion of the other. Which leads to . . .

LUCIA'S LAW 16

The goal of retirement planning isn't so much to get rich as it is to avoid becoming poor.

How much safety and how much growth would work for your portfolio? In part that depends on your personal makeup and your tolerance of risk.

Know Thyself

Are you the sort of person who's intimidated by all the jargon and all the decisions that go with investing? Who looks at his portfolio as little as possible—maybe at tax time and hardly at all the rest of the year? Who would sooner cut off an ear than buy anything risky? Who sleeps fitfully, if at all, when his 100 shares of Exxon drop a few points?

Or are you the kind who reads *The Wall Street Journal* for fun? Who knows the current prime rate to within an eighth of a point? Who loves being asked, "What do *you* think is going to happen to the market?" Who thinks buying Internet stocks on margin is more fun than a picnic in the park?

Perhaps you're neither of the above. Maybe you're the type of investor who isn't as much frightened as just plain bored by the markets, who finds studying his stocks about as exciting as watching grass grow. Maybe you think investing—like paper-training the puppy and cleaning the gutters—is okay as long as someone else does it. So you're inclined to delegate to anyone who shows the slightest hint that he knows what he's doing, even if that's your oft-unemployed brother-in-law.

Whatever your style, you may need to fine-tune it a bit as you head for retirement. This is a time to avoid being either foolhardy or overly cautious. And if you've used ignorance as an excuse not to get involved with your finances, perhaps retirement can be a helpful catalyst for change. Truth is, investing is not as complicated as some would make it. If you've got some patience and a willingness to learn a little, you can do well.

Lots of Possibilities

As we've already pointed out, Social Security and employer pensions probably aren't going to be enough to sustain you over a long retirement. In fact, some analysts say that for an average retiree, up to 60 percent of retirement income needs to come from his or her own investments. If so, you're going to need some investment skills, some information, and the right attitude. Ultimately, investing well comes down to having lots of information (possibilities), knowing the likelihood of something happening (risk), and having the mind-set to make the right decisions when they need to be made.

For many of us, risk evaluation is an emotional process. How you *feel* about risking your money—or conversely, how safe it must be—will affect many of your decisions as an investor. You could be ultraconservative (like the Nelsons, who didn't want to risk one dollar) or ultra-aggressive (like the Hendersons, who were ready to risk all or most of their money on the chance that it will grow wildly).

Most of us, fortunately, prefer a middle road. We want a mix of safe-but-slow investments as well as some higher-risk, higher-return possibilities.

A Fit with Your Comfort Level

Knowing something about your risk tolerance may help you make decisions that'll give you both peace of mind and a feeling of accomplishment and success. Your strategy should not be too far out of line with your comfort level. Although your tolerance for risk may rise or fall depending on lots of factors—job security, confidence about the future, investment experience—over the long run it's probably fairly consistent.

The conservative investor who goes against his or her instincts to invest heavily in penny stocks and commodities futures is probably going to feel uncomfortable no matter how well the portfolio fares. Similarly, an aggressive investor with all his or her money in savings bonds is going to be unhappy despite the so-called safety of that investment.

How Much Risk Feels Right to You?

The following, highly unscientific quiz may give you an idea of your risk comfort level. Some of the questions are finance-related, and some are more about temperament.

Don't overthink your responses. There are no wrong answers. This shouldn't be stress-inducing, but rather just a quick read on whether you might need to nudge yourself toward being a bit more bold or rein yourself in if you tend to overreact when emotions run high.

Circle the answer that most closely approximates your likely action or opinion. There's a scoring guide at the end.

A. *On days when you hear on the news that the Dow Jones takes an enormous leap, do you:*
   1. Congratulate yourself on not being a part of that game?

2. Pride yourself on having stocks for the long haul but plan to buy no more?

3. Call your broker and try to get in while the getting is good?

B. *Your investing motto, if you had one, probably would be:*

1. "A penny saved is a penny earned."

2. "Patience is a virtue."

3. "Go for it!"

C. *If you were in Las Vegas and in the mood for a game, you'd immediately head for:*

1. Bingo

2. The quarter slots

3. Blackjack

D. *You're playing tennis. It's set point, match point, and your second serve. Do you:*

1. Play it safe and hit an easy serve rather than double-fault?

2. Hit a medium-hard serve, taking into account that you could lose the game—or win it—with this shot?

3. Say to yourself, "No guts, no glory," and try all-out for an ace?

E. *You're putting in an offer to buy a house you really want. You understand there's another interested buyer also composing an offer. The asking price is $299,999. Do you:*

1. Make an offer above the full price? "This one's not going to get away."

2. Offer full price? "What could be more fair than that?"

3. Offer $285,000? "The owners can lump it or leave it."

F. *You win $500 in a football pool at your health club. Do you:*

a. Put it in an interest-bearing savings account?

b. Deposit it in your mutual fund account?

c. Try to parlay it into something bigger by buying a "hot" stock?

G. *You buy 200 shares of stock at $33. A week later, it soars to $45 on a strong profit report. Do you:*
1. Hold all 200 shares? "Why rock the boat?"
2. Sell 100 shares and look for another good, more reasonably priced stock? "Nobody ever went broke taking a profit."
3. Buy more of the same on margin? "This baby's a winner."

H. *In a single week, you get three preapproved applications for credit cards. Do you:*
1. Toss them? "I don't need more plastic. In fact, I don't need *any* plastic."
2. Decide to look them over for a while, comparing annual fees and interest rates? "A smart decision might save me a few bucks."
3. Send 'em in? "A person can't be too rich, too thin, or have too much credit."

I. *You inherit $5,000 from a long-lost uncle. That's hardly enough to alter your lifestyle, so do you decide to:*
1. Just put it in the bank and use it to help make your mortgage payments?
2. Buy a bond or a bond fund?
3. Buy a high-flying stock?

J. *The stock market turns south in a big way. So do you:*
1. Sell?
2. Decide to watch for a few months before deciding?
3. Buy at bargain prices because a quick rebound is likely?

K. *Which of the following most closely describes your feelings toward investing?*
1. Avoiding risk is more important than pursuing a high return.
2. Preservation of principal is a high priority, but I'm comfortable with some risk to improve my return.
3. I leap at above-average risk if it offers the hope of above-average returns.

L. *The way I feel generally about the future of investment mar-
    kets is:*
    1. They will always be too risky.
    2. If I'm careful, there will be opportunity.
    3. There is always lots of upside potential if you know what
       you're doing and aren't afraid to act.
M. *If the value of your mutual fund went down by 10 percent
    this year even as other funds were going up, would you:*
    1. Continue to hold it?
    2. Monitor it closely over the next year and sell if it contin-
       ued to lose value?
    3. Sell it and find one with better returns?
N. *How many months of current expenses could you cover
    without dipping into your investable assets?*
    1. Six months to a year.
    2. Less than six months.
    3. One month or less.

Scoring:

Add the numbers circled and compare to the following guide:

You scored 14–20. You're an ultra-conservative investor who
    rarely takes chances with money. Unless you have a very
    long time horizon or already control substantial wealth, you
    may want to try to nudge yourself to be less risk-averse to
    meet your retirement needs. Fear of short-term loss could
    lead you to forfeit a good deal of return needlessly.
You scored 21–30. You're a middle-of-the-road investor who
    appreciates the need to take calculated risks. This is a good
    mind-set to have when investing for retirement.

You scored 31–42. You're an aggressive investor who may get an emotional charge out of taking a risk. You need to make sure that your inclination to do *something* in times of stress doesn't lead you to make unwise choices.

So what kind of investor are you? Nervous? High-rolling? Or something in between? Whatever your instincts, you can achieve both comfort and safety with the right investment strategy.

I think *Buckets of Money* is just such a strategy. Invest your money in short-term, mid-term, and long-term "*Buckets*" and you'll likely:

- Get the safe, reliable income you want from the very first year—and continuing for many years to come, perhaps as long as you live.
- Increase your income periodically to keep pace with inflation.
- Produce a substantial portfolio that you can continue to live on, or that you pass onto your heirs.

Buckets is flexible. If your tolerance for risk is higher or lower than usual, if your need for an income stream is more or less than somebody else's, if you want to get by on less in the short term in order to reap more down the road, or vice versa, the *Buckets of Money* system can be tweaked to match your preferences.

I'll give you plenty of examples of how *Buckets* works. But they will only be that—*examples.* At the end of the next chapter, there will be a worksheet where you can plug in your own numbers. Whatever numbers you chose, I think you'll see the simple logic of this strategy. Although no one can guarantee results, the *Buckets of Money* plan may provide one of the best chances of any strategy I've seen to give you both comfort and safety.

CHAPTER 4

Buckets: The Simple, Yet Proven, System

Here's a safe gamble: I'm willing to bet that you, unlike the Nervous Nelsons or the High-Rolling Hendersons, don't want to go broke slowly *or* quickly. Am I right? *See!* What a guy!

You want to invest soundly and conservatively. You don't want to bet the farm on the short-term gyrations of an erratic stock market. But neither do you wish to invest so timidly that inflation erodes your nest egg. So how can you do both: receive income *and* get the growth that stocks and other long-term investments can bring?

That's where the *Buckets* come into play. Think of them as the short-term (No. 1, the Income Bucket), mid-term (No. 2, the Safety Bucket), and long-term *Buckets* (No. 3, the Growth Bucket). You'll want to split your money, putting some into each *Bucket*. The worksheet calculator at the end of this chapter will guide you through the fairly simple calculations.

How you divide the money will depend on (1) how much you have to invest, (2) how much income you will need to live on and when you need it, (3) how many years you will need that income for, and (4) what rate of return and rate of inflation you predict.

For the purposes of our example, let's say you, like the Nelsons and the Hendersons, have $300,000 to invest and need income of $18,000 a year. This is also the example used on the worksheet calculator, so you can follow along there if you wish. I am using a 6 percent distribution rate, which by most standards is on the high side. A 4 percent distribution would be much safer, and 5 percent would be a little more comfortable. The distribution rate also depends on the current short-term interest-rate environment. For example, a 5 percent distribution may seem awfully high when inflation is 2 percent but not so high if it's 4 percent. But let's go with these numbers, recognizing that this is just an example.

In the short-term Bucket No. 1, you need to put about $106,000 and invest that in something conservative that will produce $18,000 annually for, say, seven years. (For our example, we assume a 5 percent return for Bucket No. 1.) During most seven-year time periods, this can usually be done by investing in short-term instruments like CDs, or Treasury bills or Treasury notes with laddered maturities. Investing in an immediate annuity, or a tax-deferred annuity with penalty-free withdrawals, may also provide you with guaranteed, potentially tax-favored income for a specific period. (In Chapters 5 to 7, we go into much more detail about the kinds of investments that will be best for each bucket.)

A Key Point

A key here is that—probably contrary to what you've heard or read—you will draw down not only the interest on this Bucket No. 1

money, *but the principal, too.* (Some people have a problem with that; they've always been told that's a no-no. But, trust me, in this case, it's okay, and in fact, it's necessary to help you secure your financial future and to make the *Buckets* plan work. For example, if you put all $300,000 in an account paying 5 percent or 6 percent interest, you'll go broke slowly, like the Nelsons, as inflation erodes your purchasing power over time.) However, you will not touch the other *Buckets* until Bucket No. 1 is dry.

In the second, or safety bucket, you put $86,000, and let it grow for the seven years while Bucket No. 1 is churning out income. The Bucket No. 2 money is also invested conservatively, but can handle slightly more risk and provide more hope of reward than the money in the first bucket. In our example, we use a reasonable 6 percent figure (given 5 percent short-term money) for the return from funds in the second bucket. So at that rate, the $86,000 may grow to more than $130,000 by the time Bucket No. 1 has run dry, seven years from now. (You don't *really* let it run dry, but I'll get into that later.)

Then What?

At the end of the seven years, you pour the $130,000 into the empty Bucket No. 1. Bucket No. 2 is empty but it's eventually refilled by the future potential growth from Bucket No. 3. Meanwhile, Bucket No. 1 begins pouring out money for the next seven-year cycle.

But, remember, a major goal of the *Buckets* strategy is to keep pace with inflation. So in this next seven-year period (years 8 through 14), you will need more income to buy the same amount of goods and services. Thus, you draw $22,000 a year (instead of $18,000) for the second seven years. That represents a 3 percent inflation rate.

So far, then, you've gotten 14 years of safe income, adjusted in seven years for 3 percent inflation. But what's happening to the as yet untouched Bucket No. 3?

The Growth Bucket

Because you put $106,000 of your $300,000 in Bucket No. 1 and $86,000 in Bucket No. 2, that leaves over $107,000 for the third bucket. You're not counting on this bucket for income to live on. And you can wait a long time (up to 14 years in this example) before needing to draw on Bucket No. 3. So you can take some risk by putting that money in the stock market, real estate, and other more high-risk, high-return investments.

You'll recall from Chapter 2 that I explained how stock market risk lessens greatly with time. So putting some dough in the stock market in a broadly diversified allocation model (including some real estate investment trusts) and then ignoring it is a very sound strategy. Or, as I like to say . . .

LUCIA'S LAW 17

Ignoring the market's ups and downs can, over time, make you a pile of money.

Fourteen years should be enough time for some of the market's fluctuations to balance out. With any kind of luck, that should be long enough for you to get pretty decent returns.

The Standard & Poor's 500, the most closely followed general market index, tells us that stocks have generated better than a 10 percent rate of return over the last 70 years or so. Understand, this is *not* guaranteed. But if the stock markets and real estate are as investor-friendly in the future as they have been in the past and generate about 10 percent, the nearly $108,000 in Bucket No. 3 will have grown to more than $406,000 after 14 years. That's about one-third more money than you started with!

Managing Your Bucket Relationships

I simplified the above scenario to show how the three *Buckets* differ in their goals and how they're invested. In real life, however, the *Buckets* are not independent of one another. You don't treat them as self-contained entities to be emptied one after another.

Instead, the *Buckets* must work in tandem: income, safety, and growth. For example, let's say your Bucket No. 3 investments were growing at 12 percent, higher than the 10 percent you had projected. You could take the excess and add it to your Bucket No. 2. That would be taking money from growth (Bucket No. 3) to ensure that there's always safe money (Bucket No. 2) available for income (Bucket No. 1). Conversely, if a bear market caused Bucket No. 3's growth to slow, a sophisticated investor might even want to take money from Bucket No. 2 to replenish the growth bucket.

But here's the rule: You don't ever want an *empty* Bucket No. 2. You never want to go directly from growth (Bucket No. 3) to income (Bucket No. 1) because no one knows when the next bear market will occur. One of the worse things any investor can do is run out of safe money and be forced to liquidate stocks for income in a down market. After all, that's what got the High-Rolling Hendersons into trouble.

Regularly, probably on an annual basis, you ought to take a look at how each bucket is doing and, if necessary, reallocate among the three. Any excess from Bucket No. 3 should end up in Bucket No. 2. And any extra Bucket No. 2 money can be "banked" where it is or could flow into Bucket No. 1 to extend its life. Because bear markets typically last one and a half to two years, aggressive investors should *always* have at least a couple years' income in Bucket No. 2 if for no other reason than to tide them over through a bear cycle. However, I recommend keeping far more safe money available than two years' worth.

Also, depending on which real estate investment trusts you select to work in tandem with stocks in Bucket No. 3, you may have a built-in cushion even if Bucket No. 2 gets dangerously low. I usually use REITs that have little or no leverage. That lowers the risk and volatility substantially, but may also lower the potential return.

Making sure you have sufficient money in Bucket Nos. 1 and 2 is a way of buying time. And, of course, buying time is at the heart of the whole *Buckets of Money* strategy: The longer you can leave your money in stocks and real estate, the better your chance of earning a healthy return. And making sure you have enough income and safe money is the way you allow Bucket No. 3 to grow.

A Review

Let's go back and summarize what *Buckets of Money* may do for your retirement. First, regardless of the amount of money you have to invest, a *Buckets* plan can—if current assumptions hold true—provide you with a steady, reliable income. What's more, this income (as you empty Bucket No. 2 into Bucket No. 1) can be adjusted to keep pace with inflation. That's what I call comfort, and it's what the Nervous Nelsons failed to achieve.

Second, *Buckets* will allow you to draw your income confidently, knowing that the amounts you need to live on are coming from diversified investments, which, as you'll remember from

Chapter 2, is better than just relying on one investment source. That's what I call safety, and that's what the High-Rolling Hendersons failed so miserably at.

Third, at the end of 14 years (in our example), the strategy produces a portfolio of stocks, real estate, and other long-term investments that potentially could be worth much more than your entire original nest egg ($300,000 becoming $406,000 in our example.)

What If?

What if you have more than $300,000 to invest? You can divvy it up in ways to give you more income (putting more into Buckets Nos. 1 and 2) and/or more growth (putting more into Bucket No. 3), or if you can wait more than 14 years, you can let your third bucket continue to grow. Or if you get lucky and there's a higher rate of return or lower rate of inflation, that, too, would affect the amounts you'll have to work with. The worksheet calculator allows you to fiddle with various scenarios.

I personally like retirees to attempt to live on a maximum of 4 percent to 5 percent of their assets rather than 6 percent or more. Although the higher numbers are potentially doable, the chance for success dramatically increases as you lower your requirement for income or lower the inflation rate.

Then What?

What do you do at the end of the 14 years? Well, if you haven't rebalanced along the way, your first two *Buckets* are probably running lean, although, as discussed, you should always have at least some safe money—perhaps a couple years' worth or more on hand. But the bulk of your money will most likely be in

Bucket No. 3's stocks and real estate. So you can take your Bucket No. 3 and use this sum to:

- Start filling the *Buckets* all over again, generating an even higher, inflation-adjusted income
- Care for yourself in your last years
- Cover the costs of emergencies or large expenses
- Give to your favorite charities
- Make gifts to your children or grandchildren
- Pass on a substantial sum to your heirs after you're gone
- Spend it on anything you choose

The important thing is that as you grow older, while others may have to make do with less and less, you, having mastered the *Buckets of Money* strategy, will be potentially growing *stronger* and *more secure.*

But What about a Parachute?

You're probably thinking, "So far, so good. Sounds reasonable in theory. But what if I break an ankle and can't work for a couple months? Or a tornado takes the roof off the house and the insurance company drags its feet? Or my daughter suddenly decides to get married and wants a big wedding? Or my car goes totally kaput? I'll need money—and *quick*—but it'll all be tied up in those danged *Buckets.*"

Well, no, it won't. Those kinds of unplanned expenses *do* happen. And sometimes it isn't even a small disaster but a chance to do something enjoyable—take a brief, spur-of-the-moment vacation, say, or replace that faded carpeting before the holidays—that requires a short-term cash infusion. What you're going to need is a parachute, if you will, in case your financial plane runs into such turbulence.

This sum will be a lot smaller than a bucket—so let's call it a *"cup."* Everybody needs a cup of money stashed away. (Maybe you already have set some aside in a rainy day fund.) How big a *"cup"*? That will depend on the level and stability of your other income. If you're in a business where layoffs are common, for instance, you'll want to put more away than someone who teaches school. If you've got money coming in from, say, a pension, Social Security, or real estate, you might not need as much as somebody else whose salary is his or her sole income. Your tolerance for risk also will dictate how big your *"cup"* of money needs to be.

Usually, an emergency *"cup"* of three to four months of your normal spending needs is sufficient. This cash must be instantly accessible—not in a retirement account where you might face big taxes or a withdrawal penalty. And you don't want to have to drain money out of your three investment *Buckets*. Often, this money resides in a money market or other safe account, such as a CD or even a short-term bond fund. But the point is, when implementing the *Buckets of Money* strategy, it's just as important to select the proper vehicle for these emergency funds as it is for the sums being invested in the *Buckets*.

Most people keep their emergency fund for the rest of their life because although they may have an occasional unplanned, big expense, they don't have so many of them that this fund is depleted. Even if part of this emergency fund is used, it tends to build back up. If the investors don't have any really serious setbacks, this fund may ultimately pass on to their heirs. Thus, this money is often also referred to as a *Legacy Asset*. Ironically, the most common use of the emergency fund money is paying for long-term convalescent care.

We'll talk in the next chapter about what kinds of assets are best for your *"cup"*. But, for now, just understand that there's nothing about the *Buckets* plan that will prevent you from being able to deal with short-term emergencies. *There.* Feel better?

What's Your Plan?

Now it's your turn to figure out how to best divide your investable assets. I've used our $300,000 14-year scenario as an example on the following worksheet calculator. The tables that accompany the calculator assume you're getting ready to retire.

Remember that the goal was to provide a seven-year income stream of $18,000 annually from Bucket No.1, then in the eighth year, increase the income to cover inflation. Keep in mind that the reason I used a seven-year period for both Bucket No. 1 and another seven-year time period for Bucket No. 2 was to illustrate a very conservative approach, one that should work over just about any 14-year period. A look back at the history suggests it would take the mother of all bear markets to seriously unsettle a stock portfolio after 14 years of owning good companies and reinvesting dividends.

However, there's nothing cut in stone about the sanctity of a 14-year Bucket No. 3. A 20-year perspective for the third bucket would be even more preferable, especially if you're a conservative investor. That might allow you to sleep better.

More aggressive investors may want to use a five- or six-year time frame for each bucket. In that case, you can easily modify the numbers by funding fewer dollars in Buckets Nos. 1 and 2 and more into growth in Bucket No. 3. If the equity markets perform at historical norms, you might end up with a significantly better rate of return and a much bigger Bucket No. 3 after the first two *Buckets* are emptied.

However, for your sake, I prefer to err on the conservative side. So for purposes of this example, let's stick with seven-year *Buckets* and inflation indexing after seven years. (There's no set rule as to when to inflate your income. Some may even want an annual raise. I have found it works best to adjust every few years rather than annually because most of us don't really feel the impact of inflation in a single year. Inflation tends to creep up on you over time.) Also, it should be noted that in some instances Bucket No. 1 will need to be stair-stepped to account for other income available at a later date. For example, an individual aged 60, and two years away from receiving Social Security, may want to bolster Bucket No. 1 to support a higher income needed for the next two years, then cut back to account for the Social Security benefit. It is simple math, and any variations should be quick and easy to calculate.

We'll go into this in more detail in subsequent chapters, but understand that certain investments or investment strategies are clearly more appropriate for some *Buckets* than for others. For example, you wouldn't want to place any stocks or equity mutual funds in Bucket No. 1. It would be far too risky to draw out principal and interest from a stock portfolio that could suffer a substantial market correction without warning. Also, you would certainly not want cash investments—like CDs or money market funds—in Bucket No. 3 because they have so little long-term growth potential.

It's Your Turn

Assume you're ready to retire, then plug in your projections. You'll probably want to experiment with different amounts, time periods, and rates of return and inflation. *Good luck!*

After you've entered your specific goals and projections, you'll have a general idea of what you can realistically expect from your portfolio at retirement. Once that's done, the easy stuff is out of the way. Tackling the numerous investment options, analyzing the impact of taxes, and determining which *Buckets* are most appropriate for the various investment strategies takes a bit more work. That's next.

Plan Your Own Future With *Buckets of Money*

                                         Example   **You**

Starting point: Enter your
total current investable
assets on Line 1.   **(1)** $300,000.00   _____

Step 1: How much do you put into Bucket No. 1?

Enter your desired monthly
income.   **(2)** 1,500.00   _____

Go to Table 4.1 at the end of this worksheet. Along the left margin is the number of years. Along the top is the rate. Select the number of years you want to get income from Bucket No. 1. *Example:* 7 years (your choice: ____ years). Select the rate of return you expect to earn from risk-fee investments such as CDs, immediate annuities, Treasury bills, or money market funds. *Example:* 5 percent (your choice: ____ percent).

With your finger, follow from the
number of years you've chosen until
you're under the rate you want.
Enter on Line 3 the number
you find there.   **(3)** 70.7518   _____

Multiply the number on Line 3
times your desired monthly income
(Line 2). This is the amount you
need to put into Bucket No. 1
today. Write it on Line 4. **(4)** $106,127.70 _____

Step 2: How much do you put into Bucket No. 2?

First, calculate how inflation will affect your income needs.

Enter your desired monthly
income from Bucket No. 1
(from Line 2) on Line 5. **(5)** 1,500.00 _____

What do you think the average rate of inflation will be during the
period you selected in Step 1? *Example:* 3 percent (your choice:
___ percent).

Now go to Table 4.2.
Find the number of years you
selected in Step 1 and follow
that line across to the rate of
inflation you just chose.
Write the number you find
there on Line 6. **(6)** 1.2299 _____

Now multiply it by the
amount on Line 5. The result
is the monthly income you'll
need after Bucket No. 1
is empty. **(7)** 1,844.85 _____

Now multiply this by the
number you used in Line 3. **(8)** 70.7518 _____

The result is the amount
of money Bucket No. 2
must contain by the time
Bucket No. 1 is empty. **(9)** $130,526.46 _____

To calculate how much you need to put into Bucket No. 2 today,
figure the rate of return you can expect from conservative investments during the period you chose in Step 1. *Example:* 6 percent
(your choice: ____ percent).

Go back to Table 4.2, select the
Bucket No. 1 time period, and
follow that line across to the
rate you just entered. Write the
number you find there on
Line 10. **(10)** ÷ 1.5036 _____

Divide the number on Line 10
into the amount on Line 9.
This is how much you need to
put into Bucket No. 2 today.
Write that amount on
Line 11. **(11)** $86,809.30 _____

Step 3: How much is left for Bucket No. 3?

Enter total current investable
assets (from Line 1) on
Line 12. **(12)** $300,000.00 _____

Subtract the amount you're
putting into Bucket No. 1
today (from Line 4). Put it on
Line 13. **(13)** −106,127.70 _____

Also subtract the amount
you're putting into Bucket No. 2
today (from Line 11).
Put it on Line 14.   **(14)** −86,809.30   _____

The result is the amount you
have left over to put into
Bucket No. 3 today.
Write it on Line 15.   **(15)** $107,063.00 _____

To calculate how much you can expect this figure to grow, ask
yourself what rate of return you can expect from a diversified
stock portfolio during the two periods you'll be getting income
from Buckets No. 1 and No. 2. *Example:* 10 percent (your
choice: ____ percent).

Go back to Table 4.2, select the total time in the two periods
you're taking from Buckets No. 1 and No. 2 and follow that
line across to the rate you just entered. *Example:* 14 years (your
choice: _____ years).

Write the number you find there on
Line 16.   **(16)** 3.7975   _____

Now multiply that number by
the amount on Line 15 and
write the answer on Line 17.   **(17)** $406,571.74   _____

If your assumptions hold true, this is the amount you can expect
will be in Bucket No. 3 when you're ready to start drawing from it.

*** The result is that using our conservative assumptions and starting with $300,000, you would have a reasonably safe, inflation-
adjusted income for 14 years and an ending value of more than
$406,000 with which to start the* **Buckets** of Money *strategy all
over again.***

Table 4.1 Expected Rate of Return

Number of Years	Rate (percent) of Return							
	3	4	5	6	7	8	9	10
5	55.6524	54.2991	52.9907	51.7256	50.5020	49.3184	48.1734	47.0654
6	65.8169	63.9174	62.0928	60.3395	58.6544	57.0345	55.4768	53.9787
7	75.6813	73.1593	70.7518	68.4530	66.2573	64.1593	62.1540	60.2367
8	85.2546	82.0393	78.9894	76.0952	73.3476	70.7380	68.2584	65.9015
9	94.5453	90.5718	86.8261	83.2934	79.9598	76.8125	73.8394	71.0294
10	103.5618	98.7702	94.2814	90.0735	86.1264	82.4215	78.9417	75.6712

Table 4.2 Expected Rate of Inflation

Number of Years	Rate (percent) of Inflation								
	3	4	5	6	7	8	9	10	12
6	1.1941	1.2653	1.3401	1.4185	1.5007	1.5869	1.6771	1.7716	1.9738
7	1.2299	1.3159	1.4071	1.5036	1.6058	1.7138	1.8280	1.9487	2.2107
8	1.2668	1.3686	1.4775	1.5938	1.7182	1.8509	1.9926	2.1436	2.4760
9	1.3048	1.4233	1.5513	1.6895	1.8385	1.9990	2.1719	2.3579	2.7731
10	1.3439	1.4802	1.6289	1.7980	1.9672	2.1589	2.3674	2.5937	3.1058
11	1.3842	1.5395	1.7103	1.8983	2.1049	2.3316	2.5804	2.8531	3.4785
12	1.4258	1.6010	1.7959	2.0122	2.2522	2.5182	2.8127	3.1384	3.8960
13	1.4685	1.6651	1.8856	2.1329	2.4098	2.7196	3.0658	3.4523	4.3635
14	1.5126	1.7317	1.9799	2.2609	2.5785	2.9372	3.3417	3.7975	4.8871
15	1.5580	1.8009	2.0789	2.3966	2.7590	3.1722	3.6425	4.1722	5.4736
16	1.6047	1.8730	2.1829	2.5404	2.9522	3.4259	3.9703	4.5950	6.1304
17	1.6528	1.9479	2.2920	2.6928	3.1588	3.7000	4.3276	5.0545	6.8660
18	1.7024	2.0258	2.4066	2.8543	3.3799	3.9960	4.7171	5.5599	7.6900
19	1.7535	2.1068	2.5270	3.0256	3.6165	4.3157	5.1417	6.1159	8.6128
20	1.8061	2.1911	2.6533	3.2071	3.8697	4.6610	5.6044	6.7275	9.6463

PART III

FILLING

THE

BUCKETS

The First *Bucket:* Consistent, Sometimes Guaranteed, and Potentially Tax-Favored Income

How much risk do you want to take with your Bucket No. 1, the short-term bucket that's going to sustain you while the other two grow? Try *zero.* Here you want to take a page from the Nervous Nelsons' book and think *safety.* (Unlike the Nelsons, however, you're only putting *part* of your nest egg into ultra-conservative investments, not the whole thing.)

You don't want to worry about your monthly retirement check. Thus, you probably want to limit choices in Bucket No. 1 to only very safe investments. That means little, if any, price fluctuation and virtually no chance of losing any principal.

As we learned in Chapter 3, risk tolerance varies from investor to investor. Each person or couple will have to make their own decisions about how much risk they are willing to accept in Bucket No. 1. But the most prudent choice—and what I recommend—is that you take zero risk.

In this chapter, we're going to survey the kinds of investments that could work for Bucket No. 1 and spell out their pros and cons.

Vary Your Choices from Time to Time

Understand that those pros and cons change with the times. The attractiveness of many investments waxes and wanes depending on what's happening with interest rates and how aggressive lending institutions and insurance companies are acting at the moment. Sometimes, for example, bonds are the best choice. Other times CDs and fixed annuities may lead the pack. So what's best this year may not be best next year. This is where your financial advisor can help you make the correct bucket choices. (See Chapter 12 for ideas on how to find the right financial planner for you.)

Bucket No. 1 Possibilities

Immediate Annuity

What you want from your Bucket No. 1 is convenient and hassle-free retirement income. An Immediate Annuity Contract (IAC) is just that: It delivers a check to your door each month or automatically deposits it to your checking account on the same date, month in and month out.

An IAC is a great way to go if you don't want to deal with reinvesting interest every six months from a bond portfolio, shopping among banks for the best interest rates when your CDs mature, dealing with brokers, or, worse yet, dealing with the government. In short, IACs amount to a "no-brainer"—a very safe and dependable source of retirement income.

What exactly is an IAC?

An immediate annuity is a contract issued by an insurance company guaranteeing payments of a specific sum to a retiree each month on a specific date. This can last for either a fixed number of months, or for the rest of the annuitant's life or the life of the joint annuitants. For *Buckets* planning, of course, it typically makes the most sense to use an annuity that pays out principal and interest over a fixed number of months rather than over one's life expectancy.

For instance, if you want $1,500 deposited into your checking account on the 15th of each month for the next seven years (the projected term of our Bucket No. 1), an insurance company will ask you to pay a lump sum equal to the discounted present value of that benefit amount based on the current interest rates they are crediting. If the insurer is currently crediting 4 percent net after expenses, a $1,500 monthly payment for 84 months would call for a single, up-front premium of $109,739. In other words, your $109,739 buys you $1,500 per month for seven years, or 84 months, *guaranteed!* This includes *both* the principal and the interest. At the end of 84 months, all the money in the IAC will have been used up.

But suppose interest rates are higher, meaning the insurance company can get a better return on the lump sum you hand over. If the insurer credits a net 6 percent, then the amount required from you to fund the $1,500 payment for 84 months declines to $102,680, or about $7,000 less. So, obviously, an IAC is more attractive at some times than others. Further, some states require insurance companies to pay a state premium tax on immediate annuities, and some companies charge an expense fee. This can cause the actual return on your investment to be a bit lower than other suitable Bucket No. 1 investment possibilities. That's a downside.

But the big advantages of IACs include their imposed discipline as well as convenience. In my view, those two plusses are unmatched and may be worth a slightly lower rate of return. For ease of budgeting, IACs are hard to beat. You usually can choose the day of the month to receive your annuity payment. Thus, you can coordinate that check with your Social Security check and/or your pension checks and have all of them deposited in your bank account each month on or about the same day.

Some contend that a fixed, immediate annuity is somewhat restrictive because it requires the retiree to live on a budget. That's true. But I would argue such a limitation can be good. If Bucket No. 1 funds were readily available, you might be tempted to spend more than you should. Then you'd be forced to dip into your other buckets, and this could upset your long-term financial security. (Also, remember, our emergency *"cup"* that exists for special needs.)

Here's another advantage of IACs: You can claim your hands are tied when friends or relatives hit you up for cash. While it is indeed a noble gesture to help your "neighbor," you should keep in mind . . .

LUCIA'S LAW 18

Toss your cash into a tornado, and the chances of seeing it again are about the same as that of recovering loans to family or friends.

Sad to say, I've learned this from personal experience. (Again, remember you've got the emergency *"cup."* It's there to lend a helping hand if you need one.) But an immediate annuity can help you—with sincerity and conviction—to "Just Say 'No.'"

In truth, some immediate annuity contracts are liquid. But you don't have to advertise that fact. It's easier just to say your money is tied up in a "retirement plan" and unavailable. Over the years, I have saved many clients from bad investments in family restaurants, jojoba ranches, ostrich farms, and other ventures of dubious merit because their retirement money was "tied up" in something perceived and accepted (perhaps with disappointment) by friends and relatives as illiquid.

Another Benefit of IACs

Another major benefit of an immediate annuity in an after-tax personal account (not traditional IRAs or pensions) is something called the *exclusion ratio*. If you invest in CDs or government bonds, you are taxed on the full amount of the interest earned each year on the entire sum invested.

Because an immediate annuity pays out *both* principal and interest on a fully amortized basis, this dramatically reduces your current income tax liability. With an immediate annuity you only pay tax on the pro-rata amount of interest you receive in the year you receive it. The rest of the interest is deferred until it is withdrawn in subsequent years.

Here's an example: If you deposit $109,739 with an insurance company and receive $1,500 in monthly income payments over 84 months, you actually receive a total of $126,000 over the seven-year period, $16,261 of which is interest. If you divide the $16,261 interest by the seven years, you get $2,323 per year. That is the amount of interest you need to report each year on your tax return. In the 25 percent tax bracket, the immediate annuity will only cost you about $580 in federal taxes per year on $18,000 of income ($2,323 × 0.25). In contrast, your first-year federal tax liability on $5,000 of interest income (from, say, CDs or Treasuries) would be about $1,250.

If you were to ignore the *Buckets of Money* concept and draw a $1,500 monthly income from just the interest from a bond fund or CD, you would need to deposit $300,000 (assuming you earned 6 percent). Further, all $18,000 earned per year would be taxable, leaving an individual in a 25 percent marginal tax bracket a spendable income of $13,500. This is significantly less than the $17,420 of spendable cash you would have generated from an immediate annuity. In fact, with the IAC you'd have 30 percent more money to initially spend at retirement. Of course, with the annuity you are using principal and interest. But that's okay because Bucket No. 3 is left to grow and in most instances will more than make up for the principal exhausted in Bucket No. 1.

Annuities also help when it comes to figuring out how much of your Social Security benefits will be subject to tax. When a single individual's modified adjusted gross income (MAGI) exceeds $25,000 and a married couple's MAGI exceeds $32,000, up to 85 percent of their Social Security benefits become taxable. If you are nearing those income levels, the immediate annuity can help you stay below the threshold and save even more tax.

Let's summarize the pros and cons of IACs:

Pros
- Eases your budgeting. Safe and dependable, IACs deliver predictable income on predictable dates.
- Requires you to live within your means. By not having immediate access to your money, you might think twice about those expenditures that exceed your regular budget.
- Gives you tax advantages. You only pay tax on the pro-rata amount of interest you receive in the year you receive it; the rest is deferred until it is withdrawn in subsequent years.
- May help avoid or reduce taxation of your Social Security benefits.

- Provides a ready excuse when friends or relatives come calling with their hands out.
- Is handled outside of probate at your death.

Cons
- Forces you to live on a budget.
- May reduce your return because of expense charges and/or taxes the insurer must pay on your premium in some states.

Clearly, there are a lot of advantages to IACs. But while they are excellent investments for safety, income, and convenience, they are clearly not the only choice for a Bucket No.1. So let's move on!

Laddered-Maturity Treasuries or Laddered CDs

One of the most popular ways to structure a Bucket No.1 guaranteed-income portfolio is to ladder investments, so a specified sum matures on the date you need it each year.

If, for example, you want $18,000 annually ($1,500 per month), the first step is to set up a check-writing money market mutual fund. Once that's established, you then deposit the first year's income needs (approximately $18,000) into the fund and each month write yourself a check for $1,500. At the end of the year, when your money fund has dried up, your first CD or Treasury instrument kicks in.

In a seven-year *Buckets* strategy the idea is to ladder six fixed investments, each maturing one year apart, starting at the beginning of year 2 and ending at the beginning of year 7. After that, it's time to empty Bucket No. 2.

Certificates of deposit at your local bank are probably the easiest investments to ladder. However, U.S. Treasury securities with comparable interest rates and maturities have a slight advantage if you live in an area with a state income tax. That's because government securities (held by you personally, not in traditional IRA or pension accounts) are exempt from state income tax, but CDs are not.

Thus, your net after-tax return could be slightly higher with Treasuries. However, it may not be worth the extra effort. That's because you either have to deal with a reluctant broker, who will earn little or nothing for the effort and most likely will charge you a nominal fee to arrange the purchase. Or, you deal directly with a Federal Reserve Bank online or through the mail. Either way, the amount of additional interest you would earn is marginal. So opting for convenience may make the most sense.

Another excellent place to shop for fixed-interest laddered maturity investments is a credit union. Sometimes credit unions will offer members interest rates slightly above that of bank CDs and short-term Treasury securities. So credit unions are definitely worth checking out. But whether you use banks, money market mutual funds, short-term Treasuries, credit unions, or immediate annuities, the yields should be comparable and your principal should be very safe.

Again, let's look at the pros and cons of laddering:

Pros
- Safe and dependable.
- Flexible. You set up the schedule, and you're not forced to live on a budget.
- Tax advantages. If you chose Treasury securities, you may save on state income tax.
- Credit unions may have special rates for members.

Cons

- Some fees and/or paperwork required if you choose Treasury securities.
- Interest on CDs is not tax-exempt.

Short-Term Bond Mutual Funds

Another low-risk investment for Bucket No. 1—and perhaps the simplest to fund—is a short-term bond mutual fund. These funds invest primarily in short-term government securities that mature in one to five years. The reason they are so simple is the mutual fund company makes all the investment decisions for you.

Instead of you having to shop for CDs and Treasuries or pick the right bond investments at the right time, a portfolio manager does it for you (for a nominal fee). You simply ask the bond fund company to send you a monthly income check from the account.

Here's the way it works: The fund company withdraws the interest from your account first, and then it sells shares of the mutual fund in your account to meet your target income. Yields on short-term bond funds will be similar to CDs or Treasuries, perhaps even marginally higher depending on how seasoned the underlying bonds are in the portfolio and what happens to interest rates. If there are bonds in the mutual fund portfolio with higher-than-market yields and interest rates are inching lower, then you may even pick up an extra return by using a short-term bond fund over other, less risky portfolio alternatives. (Not that short-term bond funds are that risky, it's just that they're not guaranteed.) When interest rates are low, the yields on short-term bond mutual funds will also be lower, because as the higher-interest-rate bonds mature, newer, lower-yielding bonds are purchased, and the fund's yield declines.

While simple, easy, and potentially higher-yielding, bond funds may not produce the best result for Bucket No.1. The prices of bonds and bond mutual funds fluctuate each day based on the daily direction of interest rates. The share price of short-term bonds and bond funds fluctuate less than longer-term bond mutual funds, but they *do* change.

In periods of rising interest rates, the share price can decline faster than the benefit derived by a little higher interest rate. If this happens and shares must be sold at a loss, the return on Bucket No. 1 may become unacceptably low and shorten the length of Bucket No. 1's payout. At the end of the day a *Bucketeer* will have to choose between the absolute safety of potentially lower-yielding CDs, Treasuries, or immediate annuities and the potentially higher-yielding mutual fund whose value may decline enough to erase some of the benefit of higher initial returns.

Price fluctuation aside, there is a small chance (but nonetheless a chance) of losing principal in highly rated, short-term bonds or bond funds. It usually comes down to comparing the options at the time you are ready to invest and seeking the best yield at that time. Bonds may fit Bucket No. 1 best when interest rates are high and expected to remain reasonably stable throughout most of Bucket No. 1's payout period, rather than when rates are low with the possibility of higher rates ahead.

To recap short-term bond funds:

Pros
- Very simple to administer. No shopping required.
- Low risk. Chances of losing principal are slight.
- Similar yields to CDs and Treasuries.

Cons

- Some price fluctuation.
- Not as attractive when interest rates are low and headed upward.

These three investments—immediate annuities, laddered CDs or Treasuries, and short-term bond funds—are what I see as best for Bucket No. 1. Although there are differences among them, they all offer safe, consistent income. Further, that income stream requires relatively little effort by you to keep it flowing. So, they offer safety and security. And, after all, that's what you're seeking in Bucket No. 1.

Two Less Attractive Possibilities

Two other possibilities are worth discussing, although for reasons you'll soon see, they're not in the same league with our Big Three.

Mid- and Long-Term Bonds or Bond Funds

Brokers wanting to enhance their client's return may be tempted to opt for higher-yielding mid-term or longer-term bonds, or long-term bond mutual funds. Unlike shorter-maturity bonds, these can and often do lose principal value if interest rates rise.

Thus, I feel longer-term bonds are usually *not* appropriate as a Bucket No. 1 investment. Rising interest rates can cause your principal in a bond or bond fund to decline substantially. That's not good in any situation, but it's doubly bad when (as with Bucket No. 1) you're systematically withdrawing funds to live on. Taking money out of a declining asset base can be frightening, especially if the declining asset represents your entire nest egg.

For instance, in 1994, interest rates increased 2 percent. Most bonds and bond funds suffered a significant principal loss for the year. Although the loss was recovered in subsequent years as interest rates plummeted, retirees who were withdrawing cash from their long-term bond fund lost money on that portion of their portfolio forever. Once again in 1999, long-term bond investors lost 12 percent of their principal as interest rates rose. Remember, there's no assurance that interest rates will decline so investors can recover that loss in short order. In mid-2003, the yield on 10-year Treasuries increased from a historic low of 3.11 percent to 4.4 percent in less than two months, causing most bonds to lose significant value in a short time.

If the economy experiences an inflationary spiral like it did in the late 1970s and early 1980s, when interest rates rose consistently throughout the decade, substantial principal could be lost in bonds and bond mutual funds. Such losses hardly make retirees comfortable, especially when they see their principal disappear before their very eyes in an investment that is supposed to be safe.

What's more, remember, the *Buckets of Money* concept requires a total depletion of a conservative Bucket No. 1. That buys you time to invest for additional safety and moderate growth in Buckets No. 2 and No. 3. The only way to buy that needed time is to deplete some of your principal using Bucket No. 1 assets and reinvest Bucket No. 2 assets based on your tolerance for risk. But if you extract an income stream consisting of principal and interest from an investment that is losing value, you accelerate the loss. Or, as I have been known to say . . .

LUCIA'S LAW 19

*Drawing down an already failing asset is like
throwing water on a sinking ship—it just
goes to the bottom that much faster.*

The withdrawals mean the principal produces less interest, and as you continue to withdraw, the whole investment spirals downward. As a result, Bucket No. 1 won't last as long as you planned, and that's going to throw off your whole *Buckets* plan.

So attempting to improve the interest return on Bucket No. 1 by extending the maturities on bonds or bond funds only to gain a 0.5 to 1 percent advantage can be foolish. (However, mid-term and longer-term investments may be exactly what you're looking for in Bucket No. 2, which we'll cover in the next chapter.)

The big picture on mid- and long-term bonds and bond funds looks like this:

Pros
- Slightly higher returns.

Cons
- Can lose principal if interest rates rise.
- Can subvert *Buckets of Money* principle by forcing you to deplete Bucket No. 1 faster than intended.

A Hybrid Approach: Money Market and Bond Funds

Bucketeers sophisticated enough to handle their own investing—and willing to assume modest risk—may want to consider a hybrid approach to funding Bucket No. 1. It is not automatic like IAC payments or systematic redemptions from a short-term bond mutual fund, laddered Treasuries, or CDs. But a hybrid approach will produce a higher rate of return *most* (but not all) of the time with a measured increase in the amount of risk.

This hybrid requires some work on your part. The idea is to pair a liquid, check-writing money market mutual fund with a higher-yielding, higher-risk bond fund, REIT, or a combination of income-producing investments. The strategy is to deplete one account *or* the other, depending on what happens with interest rates.

For example, if Bucket No. 1 requires $120,000, consider placing $60,000 in a money market account and $60,000 into higher-yielding securities. The money market rates at this writing yield about 2 percent (with virtually no principal risk). A strategic income fund, high-yield bond fund, Ginny Mae (mutual) fund, or REIT yields 5 percent to 8 percent (with some potential for loss). Thus, the blended yield is over 5 percent, which is significantly higher than other typical Bucket No. 1 assets.

If interest rates are stable or moving lower, the *Bucketeer* would withdraw the principal and interest needed for the monthly budget from the higher-yielding securities by taking the interest first, then liquidating enough shares to cover the balance needed. Because income-oriented securities tend to rise in value as interest rates decline, you would actually be selling off some profits. In other words, you would be selling high when your investments have performed well.

If interest rates rise, these same securities usually will decline in value. If this happens, the investor would cease withdrawals from the declining assets and begin to take withdrawals from the safe money market account, where there is no price fluctuation. This allows the interest from the securities account to be reinvested, thus buying more shares at lower prices and potentially enhancing your return.

Inflation and the accompanying higher interest rates are often corrected within two to three years. In this example, there is ample money in the money market account to buy two to three years' worth of time before you have to tap into the higher-yield funds.

The hybrid strategy, it's hoped, would allow for a recovery as interest rates eventually float back to the start point. So by the time you begin to deplete the higher-risk fund, most or all of your principal is recovered. If interest rates don't come down within a reasonable period of time, you have the potential for some loss of principal. This hybrid approach might provide a return that can exceed the typical Bucket No. 1's short-term investment. In a *stable* interest-rate environment, the hybrid should exceed typical Bucket No. 1 investment returns by 1 percent to 1.5 percent annually. *Bucketeers* will have to decide if the potential extra return warrants the extra risk and the extra work.

Another hybrid approach for Bucket No. 1 is to use a fixed annuity (usually most appropriate for Bucket No. 2) with a high-liquidity provision and then combine Buckets Nos. 1 and 2. For example, an annuity that pays a high rate but also allows the investor to withdraw 15 percent to 20 percent per year may work great for both Buckets Nos. 1 and 2. Because fixed annuities usually pay much higher returns than short-term instruments, being able to tap into 15 percent to 20 percent of the account balances annually is tantamount to earning much higher rates in Bucket No. 1 by using liquidity in Bucket No. 2. This also will work when blended with high-yield bond funds or other bonds just like the earlier example but using a more liquid annuity in lieu of a money market fund.

So, to sum up the hybrid approach:

Pros

- Higher returns most of the time.

Cons

- Requires retiree to keep close tabs on interest rate, and act accordingly.
- Some potential for loss of principal.

The Best Strategy for You

As you can see, Bucket No.1 investing can be as simple as receiving a check each month from an insurance company or mutual fund, or it can be as complex as a hybrid strategy in which you nimbly decide which account to draw on, depending on what interest rates are doing. Your financial acumen and the time you are willing to commit to managing your investments will dictate the best strategy for you.

One of most difficult hurdles for *Bucketeers* is the concept of depleting the principal in Bucket No. 1. The old notion of never dipping into principal is logical for individuals attempting to protect their nest egg. But keep in mind that it has the opposite effect over time. Or, as I like to say . . .

LUCIA'S LAW 20

Protect at all costs the principal in your income-producing account—and you'll end up with neither principal nor income.

As inflation erodes your purchasing power, your net spendable income actually decreases. Remember, $18,000 a couple decades from now will probably only buy half the amount of goods and services it does today. Thus, you need a growing asset base in order to provide an inflation-indexed income.

Your equity-based investments (what you will have in Bucket No. 3) have the potential to grow, and your fixed investments (Bucket No. 1) don't. So you should deplete principal in Bucket No. 1 in order to allow ample time in Bucket No. 3 for equities to do what they do best. That leaves Bucket No. 2—and the next chapter.

The Emergency *"Cup"*

What about that emergency fund we discussed in the last chapter? What are good investments for that sum? And how much of a sum do you need?

The old saw (made famous by a series of television ads a few years ago) is that you need six months' salary in an insured savings account. (Not surprisingly, it was banks and savings and loans that ran those ads.) That's a bit extreme. That would mean putting many thousands of dollars there to be savaged by inflation and taxes, all the while awaiting emergencies that probably will never happen. Is that smart? N-o-o-o, I don't think so.

Three or four months is likely closer to the mark, and you probably will want to put it in a money market and/or short-term bond fund. Those would give you more flexibility than a CD (because there are no penalties for early withdrawal) and will pay more interest than a savings account. Then, if you have an actual emergency, you could write checks on the money market account first because that wouldn't trigger a capital gain or loss, which, at the very least, will complicate your tax returns. (Using the bond fund will entail a capital gain or loss, but then the bond fund pays slightly better interest.)

Money is relatively easy to borrow now, especially in a margin account at a brokerage (with its relatively low interest rates) or through a home-equity loan (interest on which usually is tax-deductible). So, depending on your risk comfort level, you could get by with even less than three months' worth of cash equivalents.

Most people keep their emergency fund for the rest of their life and hope it will outlast them and thus be passed onto their heirs. That's why I call this portion of retirement savings the *Legacy Asset*. Only a very serious situation, such as the need to pay for long-term convalescent care, would cause you to draw down on the majority of this reserve. Aside from that or a similar event, it's likely that the *Legacy Asset* will sit untouched.

The Insurance Option

As financial planners, we sometimes recommend using a special type of insurance policy for the *Legacy Asset*. Such policies can provide a growing cash value *and* access to your money in case of an urgent need as well as tax-deferred and/or tax-free death benefits.

Convalescent care, home health care, and other potential needs also may be accommodated by this type of insurance, which is available to certain qualified individuals. Careful consideration of the needs for both life insurance and long-term health care is an important part of anyone's financial planning.

Another approach comes from *The Wall Street Journal* columnist Jonathan Clements, who says he keeps only a small amount of his emergency fund in cash, with the rest going into a stock mutual fund. "By putting my emergency money in stocks, I am not just preparing for the worst. I am also preparing for my retirement." Clements figures that because of the returns earned by stocks, his emergency reserve should grow to far more than six months' living expenses and eventually add to the comfort of his retirement.

That's not for everybody, and you need to do what's right for you. But as with the *Buckets*, the strategy with your "*cup*" should be to invest smartly, with an eye not only toward return but also toward achieving the comfort that you desire and deserve in your retirement.

CHAPTER **6**

The Second *Bucket:*
A Conservative Cache
for Inflation-Indexed
Income Later

If the *Buckets* were like people, Bucket No. 1 would be Larry Lunchbox, the working stiff who scrapes and scrounges to keep the money coming in so there's food on the table and a roof over his family's head. He can't take any chances with his hard-won wages. So he focuses on the short term and on just paying his bills. His time horizon is short.

Bucket No. 2 is akin to Sammy Suburban, a Yuppie middle manager. Although not rich, he's a little more comfortable and can kick back a bit. He still needs income, of course, but he can sock some money away and let it grow. So he can take on a bit more risk than Larry Lunchbox, and if a really red-hot investment opportunity presented itself, Sammy could decide to go for it. His time horizon is medium, or five to seven years in our example.

The third bucket is more like Tommy Trustfund, a rich layabout. He has all the time in the world—and all the fun! He doesn't have to worry about tomorrow or even the next five to seven years. He can buy whatever sound investment is likely to pay the best return and then, freed of fretting about the market's ups and downs, he can watch in amazement as his wealth compounds. His time horizon is long, or about 14 years in our example, or perhaps even longer.

In the last chapter we looked at what investments work best for Larry Lunchbox's first *Bucket*. The best choices were: immediate annuities, CDs, and short-term bond funds. But what's the best bet for our Sammy Suburban and Bucket No. 2? Mid-term and longer-term investments are inappropriate for a depletion account like Bucket No. 1. But they are *excellent* for Bucket No. 2 because they usually generate a higher return over time.

Again, you neither want nor need to take excessive risks with Bucket No. 2. You'll have plenty of risk and excitement when you invest your Bucket No. 3 money. So focusing on higher-yielding *fixed-income* securities in Bucket No. 2 usually makes the most sense.

All investments are aimed at either producing income or growing in value, or both. Fixed-income securities—those designed to make regular payments to you—provide a reasonable degree of certainty that the money will be available when it is needed. They are safer than growth-oriented investments in the sense that these payments are more reliable than the hoped-for growth.

Furthermore, Bucket No. 2 can also be used to potentially enhance your overall rate of return by taking advantage of certain buying opportunities. For example, following almost every stock market correction in the last 50 years (with the exception of 1973–1974), there was a significant recovery over the ensuing six months to two years. Because we have bought ample time in Bucket No. 1, more aggressive investors may choose to divert some of their Bucket No. 2 money into Bucket No. 3 shortly after a steep stock market decline. Thus, if the market rebounds, the return on that portion invested from Bucket No. 2 could dramatically outpace the fixed or semi-fixed return of Bucket No. 2. After the rebound, one could pay back the money borrowed from Bucket No. 2 and leave the excess profits to grow in Bucket No. 3.

Remember, Bucket No. 2 exists to replenish Bucket No. 1 when it runs dry. This works something like an insurance policy. For instance, if I need $1,000 a month income today that will last seven years, I'll need about $73,000 stashed away in Bucket No. 2 (assuming it earns 4 percent). But then what do I do in the eighth year? By then, inflation most likely will have caused my need for income to increase. At 3 percent annual inflation, I'd need about $1,230 per month.

To produce $1,230 per month starting in eight years, I'd need about $90,000. So my Bucket No. 2 will need to contain $90,000 after seven years. But if I can earn, say, 6 percent on my fixed-income investments over that seven-year period, I would need to fund Bucket No. 2 with about $60,000 today. So that $60,000 is sort of insurance that after seven years I will have another seven years' worth of income.

There are many income-producing options for Bucket No. 2. Let's look in detail at a few of the best ones.

Bucket No. 2 Possibilities

Tax-Deferred Fixed Annuities

I've spent many hours analyzing the best investments for Bucket No. 2, and I've concluded that, depending on the interest-rate environment and your tax bracket, Guaranteed Investment Contracts (GICs), stable value funds (usually offered within

401(k) plans), or tax-deferred fixed annuities often make ideal Bucket No. 2 investments. But, naturally, it's a mixed bag.

First, some background. A fixed annuity is similar to a tax-deferred CD but is offered by insurance companies. They pay a fixed return that's usually higher than Treasuries, and they are typically adjusted annually or after a number of years. The annuity is sponsored by an insurance company instead of a bank, *and* taxes are deferred each year on the profits you earn. Naturally, tax-deferred money grows more quickly than money that's taxed annually.

GICs and stable value funds, which usually are available only in retirement plans, and tax-deferred fixed annuity contracts, a close cousin to the GIC offered to individuals, offer an excellent blend of both safety and reasonably high yields when interest rates are low with the potential to move higher. Having an investment that performs well in a rising interest-rate environment is a great way to protect against interest-rate risk.

Conventional wisdom suggests that if you want high yields and low volatility, bonds or bond funds make the most sense. I respectfully dissent because often that's just not true. Which reminds me of an old saying that I'll label . . .

LUCIA'S LAW 21

When interest rates rise, two things can happen—and they're both bad.

The two bad effects are: Stocks usually lose value and bond prices decline. Because stocks are reserved for long-term growth in Bucket No. 3 (more about that later), a conservative *Bucketeer* may feel most comfortable with assets that offer a yield competitive with intermediate bonds but without the price fluctuation.

Unlike bonds, the yield on a GIC or tax-deferred fixed annuity usually gets better if interests rates rise. And, if interest rates decline, the GIC yields will also decline, but that's okay.

The reason that's okay is because as interest rates move lower, stock prices usually soar. Thus, Bucket No. 3 should more than make up for the lower yields on a GIC. Fixed annuities also offer tax deferral. So in a personal (taxable) account, the taxes due on the interest are deferred until after Bucket No. 1 is depleted. At that time the deferred annuity can be annuitized—that is, set up to provide a fixed sum at regular intervals. Thus, it'll produce an income to replace Bucket No. 1, and the taxes will be spread out over a period of years. If Bucket No. 2 is an IRA, pension, 401(k), or similar plan, the fund is already tax-deferred and will all be taken as ordinary income when paid out, regardless of whether you use a fixed annuity.

Even without the advantage of tax deferral, fixed annuities pay excellent interest rates, and those rates respond quickly to changing economic conditions. Currently, longer-term and higher-risk bond funds yield between 3 percent and 7 percent with the downside potential to lose principal if interest rates rise.

In contrast, many insurance companies offer fixed annuities with annually renewable interest rates in that same 3 percent to 7 percent range. Fixed annuities usually earn rates near those of 10-year Treasuries, or in some cases even above them. However, if interest rates inch upward, the credited rate on a fixed annuity contract would most likely renew at the higher market rate. And unlike 10-year Treasuries or other bonds, there is no downside principal risk. But there's no upside appreciation either if interest rates decline.

Thus, when interest rates are low, with the potential to move up, a fixed annuity is superior to a bond or a bond fund. When rates are high with the potential to move down (and if you can predict when interest rates will go up or down, let me—and the rest of the world—know), bonds may be a better choice.

Fixed Annuities: A Great Complement to Stocks

I like fixed annuities because they are a great complement to a well-diversified stock portfolio, especially when interest rates are on the rise. However, many financial pundits and self-proclaimed money experts constantly beat down annuities as an investment. The reason: Most insurance company products are not understood.

Fixed annuities, unlike variable annuities, are no-frills investments. They usually do not have extra fees or charges (outside of a nominal contract charge) and no out-of-the-ordinary expenses. They do not provide any upside potential like variable annuities, no death benefits to speak of, and no potential to shift from safety to growth with one easy phone call. All the profit the insurance company makes on the sale of fixed annuities is priced into the interest rate they credit. If you don't like the rate, you don't buy the contract. Fixed annuities are like tax-deferred CDs paying a fixed, usually high-yielding interest rate. As long as investors understand they are buying a contract that shouldn't be touched for five to seven years due to a surrender penalty and until after age 59½ due to federal and state penalty taxes, they usually can enjoy the higher returns and the comfort of having those returns pegged to market interest rates.

I sometimes favor GICs or fixed annuities that lock in the rate for five to seven years instead of one in which the rates change annually, especially if I really like the rate and that rate can comfortably achieve my objective. This way the insurance company can't entice you with a high rate in the first year, then once you're locked in, lower it to enhance the firm's profit. However, it's hard to beat a fixed annuity with a competitive floor rate (the rate cannot drop below the floor rate regardless of the interest-rate environment) offered by a company that offers its renewal clients the same rate as its new customers.

A question commonly asked is how can insurance companies offer competitive, bond-type interest rates and little or no price volatility? The answer is insurance companies are in the business of assuming risk in return for guarantees. They take your investment dollars, guarantee a return consistent with the yield on most mid-term, fixed-income securities, and then they invest the money in higher-yielding, longer-term investments (assuming the interest-rate risk and the investment risk themselves). Insurance companies have massive distribution forces, including agents, brokers, direct salespeople, and direct distributors. They are constantly bringing in new capital to be invested. Thus, going out longer on the yield curve to achieve a higher interest rate for their customers or investing in mortgages or private placements is not as risky for them as it is for you and me.

Insurance companies can (with few historic exceptions, such as Executive Life of California Insurance Company or First Capital) weather interest-rate cycles. If interest rates rise, they use new money to fund any current needs for capital and leave the older investors alone. (By the way, GICs and fixed annuities are not a Ponzi scheme, in which early investors are paid off with proceeds from the more recent ones. Instead, insurance companies use their entire portfolio to back their fixed annuities.) In addition, because of a draconian surrender penalty, insurance companies know they will keep your money for the length of the contract term and don't have to worry about liquidity for years. This enables them to make more money for themselves and in turn give you more.

Many insurance companies' fixed annuities have constantly exceeded the rates of return credited on five-year CDs and 10-year Treasuries by 0.5 percent to 1 percent or more. These products have long-term track records to prove their competitiveness over the past 10, 15, and 20 years. This makes fixed annuities an excellent option for Bucket No. 2.

Why Are Fixed Annuities Hated?

If fixed annuities and GICs pay interest rates competitive with high-rated bond funds and without the volatility, why do so many financial pundits despise them? For one thing, many critics confuse fixed annuities with variable annuities, which offer a family of tax-deferred separate accounts similar to mutual funds under the umbrella of an insurance contract.

Variable annuities are more complex investment vehicles that offer a number of benefits for a price. Many financial pundits do not understand the value you receive for the fees charged in a variable annuity, and some variable annuities should be avoided at all costs. Later, I'll discuss where variable annuities may fit and where they don't.

Some individuals complain that annuities create a lot of ordinary income and no capital gain, which is taxed at lower rates. This is true. Both fixed and variable annuities defer the gain, which is taxed at ordinary-income rates when the money is withdrawn. However, fixed annuities are invested in Bucket No. 2 for safety, not necessarily for growth, and the earnings are meant to be spent within a few years, not accumulated over time. So the fact that there is an ordinary-income hit is less significant than the reason you buy them, which is to have a *safe,* high-yielding investment.

For reasons that elude me, some uninformed investors don't like to deal with insurance companies. Maybe that's because there are some products sold by unscrupulous insurance agents that are perceived to be inappropriate. But there are good and bad apples in every business, including the investment world. Those bad apples should not brand fixed or variable annuities as bad. When interest rates are relatively low and the risk of owning longer-term bonds is high, then a fixed annuity might be a great solution. The only downsides of a fixed annuity are the surrender charge, the pre–age 59½ penalty, and the possibility that if the insurer went broke, your money could be lost.

The surrender charge is the way insurance companies recover their costs if you surrender the contract before it expires. Invest for five to seven years, and you earn a high return. But if you bail out early, you may have to pay a declining fee (for example, 6 percent after one year, 5 percent after two years, 4 percent after three years). Of course, if you bail out of a five-year CD, there's "a substantial penalty for early withdrawal." Where's the difference?

The pre–age 59½ penalty is irrelevant if you plan on spending your annuity money after you retire (post–age 59½). But what about the risk that the insurance company could go belly up and take your dough with it? Although that's very unlikely and has happened only a few times in history, it does mean you need to choose solid companies, as you would want to do with any investment.

Some also argue against GICs or fixed annuities because a broker receives a commission if you buy one. But if you have enough income coming in from Bucket No. 1 and the interest rate being offered by the insurer on your fixed annuity in Bucket No. 2 is higher than other safe alternatives, why should you care? If a broker earns a commission for having sold you an excellent product, so what? Remember, the commission on most fixed annuities is already priced into the return, and there usually are no loads to deal with. So, again, if you like the yield, go for it. Commissions of equal or greater amounts are also paid on brokered CDs and most bond funds. And unlike bond funds, GICs and fixed annuities usually don't charge an ongoing management fee of 0.5 percent to 1 percent per year.

Be careful, however, because for the sake of a higher commission, some not-so-professional advisors representing marginal companies may attempt to bait you with high rates in the early years, locking you into lower rates in subsequent years, and you can't get out because of a long-term surrender penalty. This type of fixed annuity should be avoided and so should the broker. Well-chosen fixed annuities sold by honest financial advisors through excellent companies can be great, safe investments for Bucket No. 2, although not always and not for everyone. To summarize:

Pros
- Usually higher-yielding than CDs and Treasuries.
- Interest is tax-deferred.
- Principal is guaranteed.
- Interest payments usually increase if market interest rates rise.
- Complements well-diversified stock portfolio.

Cons
- Interest payments usually decrease if market interest rates fall.
- Surrender charge levied if you cash in early as well as a tax penalty if you cash in before age 59½.
- Could face loss of principal if company folds.

Bonds

Bonds and bond funds really shine in some eras. For example, in the inflation-ridden 1970s and 1980s, when interest rates were high with the possibility of moving lower, bonds were an especially good choice. More recently, as the stock market imploded beginning in the year 2000 and the Federal Reserve began lowering interest rates, most bonds and bond funds posted magnificent results.

And what is a bond? A bond is a loan. It can be a loan to the government, a loan to municipalities, a loan to high-rated corporations, or a loan to low-rated or unrated companies or foreign entities. The yields, or rates of return, on all of these loans vary, depending on (1) the creditworthiness of the borrower and (2) the time remaining until the loan is either called or it matures and is paid off.

Among the bond options for Bucket No. 2 are corporate bonds, EE savings bonds, Series I bonds, TIPS (Treasury Inflation-Protected Securities), junk bonds, preferred stocks, Ginny Maes, tax-free municipals, and even REITs (real estate investment trusts). REITs are not a loan, but, like bonds, are a high-yield investment; we'll cover them in detail later. Also, some variable annuities also may qualify. Bonds pretty much pay a fixed return for a specific time and upon maturity your principal is returned.

Loans to risky borrowers and those with the longer maturities offer the highest yields. The safer and shorter loans usually yield significantly less than longer-term and riskier bonds. Bonds come in all kinds of shapes and sizes. Some quick definitions are in order:

- Corporate bonds, of course, are loans to businesses. Junk bonds are high-yield (low- or unrated) corporate bonds, which carry a higher interest rate in exchange for greater risk.
- Preferred stock pays fixed and generally higher dividends than common stock and also trades at a price that's usually more stable than common stock.
- Ginny Maes—or more properly, Government National Mortgage Association Pass-Through Certificates—are the highest-

yielding government securities and provide mortgages for homebuyers.

- Series I bonds provide a fixed return and a supplemental return tied to inflation.
- TIPS are government bonds that increase in value during inflationary times.
- Tax-free municipals are, just as they sound, loans to state and local governments, the interest on which is not taxed by the federal government and not taxed by the state, either, if you live in the state where the bonds are issued.

For more details, see the Glossary.

Bond Mutual Funds

Most of these bonds, or bond-like instruments, can be bought singly or as part of a mutual fund. Many retirees prefer not to deal with individual bonds because:

- Trading individual bonds in small lots can get expensive.
- Small investors usually don't have access to the best bonds at the best prices.
- If individual bonds are redeemed or called before they mature, reinvestment decisions are required. That's something retirees may not want to deal with.

Thus, there is more management associated with purchasing individual bonds. Plus, there's always the potential risk of default, or the risk that a certain event could cause a rapid depreciation in a bond's value. (You may remember Dow Corning's breast-implant disaster, Johnson & Johnson's Tylenol scare, California's Orange County default, or other situations that affected the value of some individual bonds.) U.S. government bonds are, as a practical matter, not subject to default.

The advantages of bond funds include:

- Professional management and diversification.
- Bond fund managers usually can purchase the best bonds at the best prices due to the fund's size, economies of scale, and research capabilities.
- Even if one or two bonds in a bond mutual fund run into problems, the yield and price of the overall bond fund only will be marginally affected. So the investor needn't worry about default risk having a substantial negative impact on most bond funds.

Bond mutual funds come in several flavors. Open-ended funds, closed-ended funds, and unit investment trusts (UITs) are the most common. Open-ended funds offer an unlimited number of shares forever. Thus, you can redeem your shares with the mutual fund company when you want the money. A closed-end fund sells only a certain number of shares. Thus, its shareholders must negotiate with other investors to sell their shares, which means the price received can be—and usually is—less than the quoted market price. UITs are groupings of bonds that are selected for similar maturity dates and interest rates, then held until maturity. When a given bond in the UIT matures, your pro rata share of the proceeds is returned to you.

Open-ended bond mutual funds are excellent in terms of providing consistent, competitive returns, but they do have one drawback. When you buy an individual bond, you know exactly when the bond matures. Therefore, you have little downside risk if you hold the bond until maturity.

When you buy an open-ended bond fund, there is no definite date of maturity. There is an *average* maturity of the bonds in the portfolio, but no date when all bonds are paid off and all capital returned. In fact, if the average maturity of a bond fund is 20 years, it is conceivable that 10 years from now, it will still have a 20-year average maturity. That's because as one bond matures, a new, usually longer-term bond is purchased. That's also why the interest-rate risk in open-ended bond mutual funds must be understood before investing. Bond funds pay interest based on the underlying loans made. The yield will change slightly as some bonds mature and the fund manager takes the cash and buys a new bond at the current market rate. These changes in yield are gradual and hardly noticeable but over time can affect your income dramatically.

What does change is the principal value of the bond fund. If interest rates rise, the value of the bond fund declines. If interest rates decline, the value of the bond fund increases. This is a good reason for sharp *Bucketeers* to use GICs when rates are low and use mid- to longer-term bonds or a hybrid when rates are high. This maximizes the performance of Bucket No. 2 while minimizing the risk.

Don't Chase Yield

There are dozens of different bond funds to consider as Bucket No. 2 assets. A word of caution: *Do not get lured into buying those with the highest yields.* Chasing yield or a hot fund in any investment is usually a recipe for disaster. Higher yields may also mean higher risk, so be careful.

Although Bucket No. 2 can tolerate some volatility, it would be a mistake to invest all of it in, say, foreign bonds yielding 16 percent only to find out that by the time the foreign currency was converted into dollars, you actually lost 30 percent. Suitable bond investments for Bucket No. 2 would be solid, well-managed bond mutual funds. This could include high yield junk and even growth-and-income funds, preferred stock, or a portfolio of several different income-oriented funds. But to stay on the safe side, it's always better to allocate the greatest percentage of your income portfolio to high-quality corporate bonds, government bonds, and Ginnie Maes.

Other Bond-Type Products

The sheer number and variety of bonds, bond funds, and Bucket No. 2-type assets can be confusing. So here's a quick rundown on some of the major kinds. (All of these—and in fact, all of the investments mentioned in this and the preceding chapter—are summarized in Table 6.1 at the end of this chapter.)

Growth and income funds split the assets between stocks and bonds. They often make more money in good times and lose more in bad times than their cousin, the *balanced fund* (which invests in all four asset classes—cash, government securities, corporate bonds, and stocks). By contrast, an *equity income fund* invests just in stocks that pay dividends.

Intermediate- and long-term government securities are one of the best ways to avoid default risks. These securities include Treasury notes, which mature in two to 10, years and Treasury bonds, which mature in 30 years. There are also Series EE savings bonds and Series I (inflation-indexed) bonds (which you generally must hold for at least 12 months), and TIPS (Treasury Inflation-Protected Securities). These all are subject to federal tax only (exempt from state tax) and, of course, are guaranteed by the federal government. The interest rates offered by all these are similar but are constantly changing. TIPs are available individually or in funds.

With *zero coupon bonds* you don't receive interest every year. Instead, you buy them at a discount to their final maturity value. You know exactly what your return will be between now and the bond's maturity date. And unlike most bonds, zeros can't be called early, and there's no default risk. U.S. Savings Bonds, for example, are really zero coupons. But the downside is that you still pay taxes on the imputed (accrued but not received) income, so holding zeros in a tax-free account may be best. Because you don't get any interest payments, there are no decisions about reinvesting the interest.

Zeros are volatile and react wildly to interest-rate changes, but if you hold them to maturity, you know exactly what you will earn. That fact can be very comforting to nervous investors as long as they focus on the final maturity and ignore the ups and downs along the way. Zeros also are available individually or in funds.

Strategic income funds seek high current income through a diversified portfolio made up largely of U.S. and foreign corporate bonds and government securities. They are "strategic" in that they're intended to help investors with long-term goals, such as college funding and retirement planning.

Foreign bond funds, naturally, hold bonds issued by other countries. But they are subject to the same foreign currency risk as international stocks.

Utility bond funds invest in bonds issued by public utilities and are relatively stable in price.

Junk bonds are high-yield corporate bonds that are rated below investment grade. Although these are the riskiest of all bonds, they are also potentially the highest yielding. Because of high default risk, the companies are willing to pay a significant interest cost for this loan. In a robust economy, many of these struggling companies succeed and pay off their debt, and the junk-bond investor wins big. If, however, the company falls, the junk-bond investor loses. Thus, junk bonds should only be purchased through a mutual fund; individual junk bonds are too risky unless you have enough money so that any one bond doesn't exceed 3 percent of your total investment.

Variable Annuities

These investments act a lot like tax-deferred mutual funds, but with a guarantee that you won't lose principal if you die. (The insurance company pays to your heirs the full amount invested if you die, even if the market suffered a decline.) They are *variable* in the sense that the return varies with the performance of the "subaccounts" you choose. If you invest in stock subaccounts, your return will reflect the stock market's performance. Similarly, a bond subaccount will mirror the bond market. The money grows tax-deferred, so you don't pay taxes on your earnings until you withdraw the money.

There are many different kinds of variable annuities. Some are very competitive for either Bucket No. 2 or Bucket No. 3. The most popular ones for Bucket No. 2 are those that give you a guaranteed rate of return of, say, 5 percent or 6 percent, or the return of the stock market portfolio held in the annuity for a specified number of years. You do pay an extra fee for this type of guarantee, and you may be forced to annuitize your guaranteed return over several years at a significantly lower interest rate if you elect the fixed return. So your effective return may be more like 3 percent or 4 percent instead of the 6 percent guaranteed. But during periods when stocks are producing dismal returns and you are particularly faint-hearted, your Bucket No. 2 will remain safe and earn at a reasonable rate while you sleep comfortably. On the other hand, when stocks produce better returns, you get the greater of the two. Thus, if stocks go up, you get the returns of the stock market, and if stocks decline in value, you are pro-tected with a guaranteed floor rate.

The downsides to variable annuities are that your money is locked up and also is subject to a surrender charge, management fees, and mortality and expense charges. Sometimes these fees can be high (although there are many variable annuities with sig-nificantly lower fees) or with benefits well worth the fees you pay. Also, your money is subject to pre–age 59½ penalties, so you don't want a variable if you plan on touching the money before that magic age. Further, when you pull money out of a variable annu-ity, the earnings are taxed as ordinary income even if most of the gains came from capital appreciation. Once again, in Bucket No. 2 this is okay because you will be spending this money.

Although they are insurance products, variable annuities are really just another way to buy investments on a tax-deferred basis. They work particularly well if you are in a high tax bracket during your accumulation of assets and a lower tax bracket when you begin taking distributions. In fact, one recent study by the big accounting firm of PricewaterhouseCoopers ("Variable Annuities and Mutual Fund Investments for Retirement Planning: A Statistical Comparison") concluded that variable annuities will outperform the identical returns of mutual funds long term, given a high tax bracket before retirement and a lower bracket post-retirement. This is true even after the added costs of mortality and expense charges.

It should be noted that variable annuities are far less attractive under the 2003 tax legislation. Many stock dividends will be taxed at a maximum federal rate of 15 percent, and long-term capital gains also will be taxed at a 15 percent maximum. That makes a variable annuity's gain, taxed at ordinary income rates, less desirable in a personal account.

A variable annuity with all the bells and whistles may be a more than an adequate Bucket No. 2 or 3 investment. However, you should also consider tax-managed equity portfolios and real estate. I'll cover those later.

Variable annuities are like an individual retirement account in that any withdrawals prior to age 59½ are subject to a 10 percent IRS penalty. Annuities do not enjoy a stepped-up tax basis at death, although many companies are adding tax-free death benefits to make annuities even more attractive.

Just as there are good and bad mutual funds and good and bad advisors, there are good and bad annuities. A well-trained financial planner can help you decide whether a variable annuity will work for you, and if so, which one. However, as previously stated, these are complex investments that are constantly changing. They are definitely getting better and are well worth looking into. You'll need to do your homework here, but don't throw the baby out with the bath water just because you may have heard insurance firms are ogres or variable annuities are bad. Sometimes they are a perfect fit, and sometimes they don't fit at all.

As you can see, there are a lot of different ways to play the bond or quasi-bond game for Bucket No. 2. Here's an overall look at the advantages and disadvantages of bond-type products:

Pros
- Pay fixed income.
- Return principal.
- Diversification and professional management easily attained in a bond fund.
- Potentially higher returns and a possibility of a floor with variable annuities.

Cons

- Interest-rate risk to principal.
- Active management required by holders of individual bonds.
- Some default risk with nongovernment bonds.

What makes the entire *Buckets of Money* strategy work so beautifully is that Bucket No. 1 buys you time to be a little more aggressive with Bucket No. 2, and Bucket No. 2 buys you time to go for the growth in Bucket No. 3. But I know that the names and descriptions of some of these investments can be confusing. Table 6.1 lists all the options we've talked about so far and rates them on a scale of 1 to 5 as to their risk, return, liquidity, and tax efficiency and indicates for which *Bucket(s)* they are most appropriate. (Just to be clear 1 means *lowest* risk, yield, liquidity, tax break, and total return, and 5 means *highest*.)

Table 6.1   Best Bets for Bucket No. 1 and Bucket No. 2

Type of Investment and Appropriate Bucket(s)	Risk	Yield	Liquidity	Tax Break	Total Return
Certificate of deposit (Buckets No. 1, 2)	1	2	4	0	3
Immediate annuities/GICs (Bucket No. 1)	1	2	1	3	3
Tax-deferred fixed annuities/GICs (Bucket No. 2)	1	4	2	4	4
Intermediate- and long-term government securities (Bucket No. 2)	3	3	3	2	4
Tax-free municipal bonds (Bucket No. 2)	3	3	3	5	3
GNMAs/mortgage bonds (Bucket No. 2)	3	3	3	2	3

Table 6.1 *(continued)*

Type of Investment and Appropriate Bucket(s)	Risk	Yield	Liquidity	Tax Break	Total Return
Zero-coupon bonds (Bucket No. 2)	4	3	2	2	3
Preferred stocks (Bucket No. 2)	4	4	3	1	4
Series I bonds (Bucket No. 2)	1	2	3	2	3
EE bonds (Bucket No. 2)	1	2	3	2	2
TIPS (Bucket No. 2)	1	3	3	2	3
Closed-end bond funds (Bucket No. 2)	3	4	3	1	3
Short-term bond funds (Bucket No. 1)	2	2	4	1	2
Mid- or long-term bond funds (Bucket No. 1, 2)	4	3	4	1	3
High-yield junk bonds (Bucket No. 2)	5	5	3	1	4
Strategic income funds (Bucket No. 2)	4	5	3	1	4
Foreign bond funds (Bucket No. 2)	5	5	2	1	4
Growth and income funds (Bucket No. 2)	4	5	3	3	5
Utility funds (Bucket No. 2)	4	5	3	3	4
Equity income funds (Bucket No. 2)	5	5	3	3	5
Balanced funds (Bucket No. 2)	4	5	3	3	5
Variable annuities (stock accounts) (Bucket No. 3 only unless with guaranteed floor)	4	4	2	3	4
Variable annuities (bond accounts) (Bucket No. 2)	3	3	1	3	2

CHAPTER 7

The Third *Bucket:* Investing for Long-Term Growth

Congratulations! You've made it to Bucket No. 3, where you have a chance to see some *real* growth in your nest egg, provided, of course, you think long term and you think diversification.

The ultra-conservative Bucket No. 1 will provide you income. The moderately conservative Bucket No. 2 will churn out yet more inflation-indexed income with which to replenish the first *Bucket*. The riskier Bucket No. 3—reserved for stocks and other long-term investments—aims for long-term appreciation.

Once you set up Bucket No. 3, you're going to enjoy a liberation. Why? Because unlike most stock-market investors, you're going to be firmly focused on the long term (14 years in our example, but you could choose, say, 10 years or 8 years if you're a very aggressive, or 20 years if you're an ultra-conservative investor).

The key to successful stock market investing, you'll remember from Chapter 1, is not when you invest or even which stocks you buy—but for *how long* you invest and *how diversified* you are. Given a long enough time frame and proper diversification, this Bucket No. 3 ought to be where you get the biggest bang for your investment buck.

What Is a Stock?

If a bond, as we said in the last chapter, amounts to a loan by an investor to a firm or to a government, a share of stock represents ownership. You, the investor, own a very small portion of the company—you have *equity* in it. Whereas with a bond you expect to get your money back, plus interest, you don't know with equities how much, if anything, you're going to receive when you sell.

That's a risk: You may get back less than what you paid for the stock. But many investors are willing to take that risk because the long-term trend—if you own stocks in good companies—has been upward. Further, even if all your stocks don't do well, the most you can lose is 100 percent of your investment. But your potential gains (unlike those with bonds) are potentially unlimited.

More specifically, advantages to investing in the stock market include:

- *Stocks appreciate.* That is, they can grow in value. A company that does well, or is widely expected to do well, may see its share price rise.
- *Some stocks pay dividends.* This is akin to the interest paid by bonds, although neither as high nor as predictable. The average dividend yield is now less than 2 percent. That's not a lot, but if reinvested back into stocks, it will spur your portfolio's growth.

- *Stocks are tax-favored.* Interest—from bonds, CDs, bank accounts, and so on—is taxed by the federal government at ordinary income rates as high as 35 percent. Stock dividends are taxed by the feds at a current maximum rate of 15 percent. But when you sell a stock that's gone up in value, your profit is taxed as a *capital gain.* And if you've owned the stock for more than a year, that capital gain is taxed at a maximum rate of 15 percent. What's more, you pay no capital gains taxes *until* you sell. And when you die, the capital gains that have accrued in your stocks pass on to your heirs tax-free.

- *Stocks are a hedge against inflation.* Stocks historically have grown more quickly than inflation. This is very important for our long-term *Bucket,* Bucket No. 3.

Incidentally, I'm going to give you a lot of investing basics in this book. But if you want to explore that general topic further, I heartily recommend Jordan Goodman's books, especially *Everyone's Money Book* and his book of financial definitions. He clearly and fully tells how to maximize returns on cash, pick individual stocks, select mutual funds, invest in bonds and real estate, and much more that's helpful to the individual investor. His books—and other reading recommendations—are listed in Appendix A.

The core of the *Buckets* philosophy, of course, is letting that third *Bucket* grow. While you spend safe money from Bucket No. 1 and accumulate semi-safe money in Bucket No. 2, you can leave your Bucket No. 3 alone for a number of years. This was particularly important during our most recent bear market, which began in March 2000 and was further complicated by the financial trauma caused by terrorism.

With a 12- to 14-year time horizon for Bucket No. 3, even a grizzly bear shouldn't cause you too much concern. By being a long-term investor you can blissfully ignore the "BUY THIS STOCK NOW!" headlines that leap out at you from newspapers and magazines. You can just smile when your pal at work suggests a "can't miss" stock. You can cleanse your mind of all the gloomy talk about a looming recession or the hopeful chatter about a possible boom. No more biting your fingernails and debating, "Should I get in? What if it hasn't bottomed yet?" or "Should I sell? What if it hasn't peaked yet." You won't care. You will have parked a big chunk of your money in Bucket No. 3 and will leave it there for years.

The key, of course, is getting it parked in the right places and in the right amounts and having a knowledgeable person keep an eye on it. There's no way around it, that takes expertise. All but the most sophisticated investors are going to need help.

You're going to want to pick an able financial advisor. Why? Because the truth is, by the time important financial information—for example, a certain mutual fund manager is buying value stocks even though the fund is nominally oriented to growth—gets to the general public, it's too late. You need an advisor whose antenna is finely attuned to such changes. It may help if he or she has been around for awhile and is a CERTIFIED FINANCIAL PLANNER™ (CFP®), a Chartered Financial Analyst (CFA), a Chartered Financial Consultant (ChFC), a Certified Public Accountant (CPA), or a Chartered Life Underwriter (CLU) and registered as an investment advisor. (It's okay if the advisor isn't designated quite yet as long as he or she is working toward a designation or is teamed up with someone who is designated.) But it takes more than a designation to be a good advisor. It takes some brains, some experience, some strategy, and *a lot* of integrity.

Really good advisors are hard to come by. When you find one—somebody who cares more about your financial well-being than his or her own—then you'll be able to sleep well at night knowing your portfolio is diverse and its volatility will be held to a minimum.

Because picking such a person or team is so important, Chapter 12 will go into great detail about how to find such an advisor. Meanwhile, let's look at some of the issues and the nomenclature you should first be familiar with so you can work with your advisor to best tailor a Bucket No. 3 for you.

Individual Stocks versus Mutual Funds

As you know, owning many stocks is safer than having just one or just a few. Understand, though, that owning a portfolio of stocks, rather than a few, reduces the likelihood that you're going to get rich quick. But getting rich quick is *not* what we're trying to do; we're just trying to get rich over the long haul. Or, as I like to say . . .

LUCIA'S LAW 21

Stock market investing isn't about achieving perfection.
You need good—but not spectacular—
results to do well long term.

So how do you diversify the stocks in your Bucket No. 3? Well, you can buy stocks of a bunch of individual companies. But I don't recommend that.

Doing the necessary research is very tedious. And, statistically and psychologically, it's an uphill slog: You're not likely to do as well with individual stocks. Equally important, if you go the individual stock route, you've still got to deal with the emotion of picking them and figuring out when to sell them and learning to ignore tips from friends and e-mails from stock-touting sharpies who say they have an inside track on a hot deal.

Life is simpler—and likely more profitable—if you forget about individual stocks for Bucket No. 3 and instead stick with mutual funds. But if you *must*—if you crave the adrenaline or the sense of ownership or whatever it is that makes individual stocks ring your bell—then by all means use your financial advisor as a sounding board before you invest in those. Yes, you'll have to pay a commission or fee to discuss your choices, but it'll be worth it. (And those commissions are negotiable.)

Most *Bucketeers,* however, would be far better off as mutual fund or managed account investors. A mutual fund is an investment company that pools your money with that of thousands of other investors and employs a professional manager to buy various securities, of which you then own a fraction. The price of your mutual fund shares (called the *net asset value,* or NAV) rises or falls daily with the market value of the securities held by the fund.

The fund's profits (or losses) are distributed to the investors on a pro rata basis. So putting your money in a mutual fund means you own a small piece of probably scores or even hundreds of individual stocks rather just a few—it's instant diversification.

In addition to diversification and professional management, other benefits of mutual funds include: (1) The fund handles the paperwork; (2) it's easy to get information about a fund (most have toll-free 800-numbers); (3) it's easy (sometimes *too* easy) to switch money within fund families if your goal or the fund's performance changes; and (4) the fund usually keeps tabs on the tax situation.

The fund also automatically reinvests the dividends and capital gains. Which brings me to the next point: How do mutual funds make you money? Although there is no guarantee your mutual fund will produce profits over the long run, most do. The profits come as the underlying value of the businesses (companies the fund owns stock in) appreciates in value. As the businesses become more successful, their stock increases in value— and the mutual fund value grows as well. So one way you, the mutual fund investor, can make money is by selling your shares at a profit. (But that's not something you're going to want to do soon in the life of Bucket No. 3; you're going to let those profits grow.)

Your mutual fund also may grow from your share of the dividends received quarterly from its pool of stocks and from capital gains distributions made once a year. Capital gains mean the profits in excess of losses on the sales by the fund manager of securities in the portfolio. So although you may not be selling your fund shares, the manager will be selling and buying shares in various companies as he or she tries to best position the fund. Once a year the profit or loss (usually in December) from those transactions is split among the investors. (The bear market of 2000–2003 meant many funds booked losses that they will carry forward, meaning the funds won't be distributing capital gains for some time. That's a plus for you, tax-wise.)

Again, the two ways your fund shares can grow are through your dividends and through profitable transactions made by the fund manager on stocks that have appreciated. Understand, though, a mutual fund is not like a CD or bond that cranks out a preordained return. Even the best funds do not always grow each year. A bad year for the market in general may translate to a bad year for the fund's holdings. Or the market may have a good year, but the portion of the market targeted by your fund (for instance, small-cap growth or large-cap value stocks) may be down. Or regardless of the market trend, the manager may just make poor decisions and end up with capital losses instead of capital gains.

Thus, with funds as with individual stocks, there is a risk, and there is no guarantee. But I believe if you properly diversify, rebalance, and invest for the long term, you could minimize that risk.

How to Select the Right Funds

Funds have lots of advantages. But they also have a staggering variety of objectives and philosophies. You're really not diversified if you have a bunch of funds that all own the same—or many of the same—stocks. You need funds that have different goals, different operating styles, and different managers.

For purposes of Bucket No. 3, you probably want what's generally classified as a *stock mutual fund* as opposed to one that invests in government securities, municipal bonds, foreign currencies, or the like. Because you're going to let this *Bucket* grow for years, you aren't so worried about risk (which will diminish with time) or being tax-free (which will reduce your returns). Getting *growth* is what's important for this *Bucket*. Getting tax-managed growth is even better!

Yet with thousands of stock mutual funds to choose from (many with confusing names and equally opaque objectives), choosing the right ones takes a little time and effort. Here are some factors to look at as you compare funds.

Net Asset Value

This is what it costs to buy one share in the fund. This is derived by dividing the total value of all the fund's holdings by the number of the fund's outstanding shares. Tracking Net Asset Value (NAV) lets you know if the value of your investment in the fund is going up or down. You can find this figure in the newspaper or on the Internet every day.

Total Return

This shows changes in the prices of the shares plus the results of investing the income and dividends as well as any capital gains or losses after expenses. This is the best figure to use (as opposed to yield, which is the amount the fund is paying to shareholders) when comparing one fund to another. The total return figures for one, three, and five years, as well as from the beginning of the current year, can be found in financial publications or obtained through the fund directly. (Another excellent source is *Morningstar,* a weekly reference service that comprehensively tracks the record of all mutual funds. Its web site is *www.morningstar.com.*)

Look at the total return over a long period that includes both bull and bear markets. Also be sure the money manager who achieved the good result is still managing that particular fund. You may find that some of the best funds never are No. 1 in any year but do better than the overall market in up years and lose less than the overall market in down years.

Fees

There are two kinds of fees: sales fees and management fees. You will want to know if a fund is a *load* or a *no-load* fund. (Load means it charges a sales commission.) There's no evidence that load funds perform better. In fact, as I often put it . . .

LUCIA'S LAW 22

A load is a marketing cost, nothing more and nothing less. It won't make a bad fund perform better or a good one perform worse.

So it comes down to this: If you don't need help selecting a fund, you're probably better off saving the sales fee and choosing a no-load. However, in a backhanded way, load funds may actually have an edge. That's because . . .

LUCIA'S LAW 23

A load may help you do the right thing for the wrong reason: If it keeps you from jumping from fund to fund, it's worth the cost.

In other words, if having to pay a load effectively makes you into a buy-and-hold investor, hallelujah! Being a tightwad has made you do the right thing.

In addition to the load, every fund—load or no-load—charges a management fee. A typical fee is 0.5 percent to 1 percent or more. (Some higher-risk funds, like small cap or emerging international market funds, may charge 1.5 percent to 2 percent. Those funds, if selected at all, should be added to your portfolio in small doses because they are very risky in addition to being costly.)

Turnover Rate

This is the dollar amount of stocks sold by the fund manager relative to a fund's total assets. High turnover rates mean high commission costs and large capital gains distributions, which in turn mean higher taxes. Many well-run funds have turnover rates of 30 percent to 50 percent. However, there are sometimes good reasons for high turnovers, such as the funds being tax-managed. Again, *Morningstar* and a good advisor can help explain a fund's turnover rate and whether it's reasonable.

Size

This tells you the amount of assets the fund manages. A fund that's too small may incur higher administrative costs. A good rule of thumb might be to avoid any fund that's stuck at the $50 million level or below for several years. If it hasn't grown, it may be because its lackluster performance has attracted few new investors.

Beta

This is a fund's volatility compared to market as a whole (with the market = 1.0). With a beta higher than 1.0, the fund fluctuates more than the market as a whole. With a beta below 1.0, just the opposite.

Manager

It's not a bad idea to look for a manager (or a group of managers) who has been with a fund—or at least, the fund family—for a few years. Nonperforming managers tend not to last long. *Morningstar* also provides lots of information about managers.

How Many Funds Should You Own?

If you—by yourself or with an advisor—find funds that look good, the question becomes: How many do you buy? There's no hard-and-fast rule about this, but common sense plays a part. An accepted view is that seven or eight is probably as many as you can regularly track and enough to achieve the proper diversification. I normally recommend a large-cap growth, a large-cap value, a small-cap growth, a small-cap value, an international, an emerging markets, and a real estate fund. If large is really large and small is micro, then adding a mid-cap growth and a mid-cap value fund would be okay.

Remember, your aim is to cover a number of different aspects of the market with funds that will do well during different parts of the economic cycle. You want funds that don't all march to the same drummer. Some (those concentrating on financial services stocks, for example) do better in periods of high growth and low interest rates while others (such as those including pharmaceutical stocks) may outperform during down times. You want to have all the bases covered.

How to Get Diversified

What makes Bucket No. 3 really work is broad diversification and a multi-asset, multi-style, multi-manager approach to investing the money. How do you get that kind of team of money managers working for you? Well, you're going to need to hire a financial advisor who is up to date on asset-allocation strategy and who can work with a money-manager selection firm to help pick good fund managers and continuously monitor their performance relative to risk. Your advisor will hold those managers to their style discipline (growth, value, large-cap, small-cap, and so on.) And if your advisor is good, he or she won't be afraid to terminate those managers who consistently underperform relative to their benchmarks.

I can't stress enough how critical it is that the money managers do not overlap in terms of their investment styles. If you have a large-growth manager, for example, who, when value stocks get hot, starts gravitating toward value in order to pump up his or her results, that's going to leave you underinvested in growth stocks. It's also going to set you up for a fall.

A classic case of this was in the year 2000 when tech stocks were riding high after several years of phenomenal gains. A lot of nominally nontech managers lusted for some of those tech stocks to bolster their portfolios. (There's intense competition among managers to get quarterly results that'll make their fund stand out.) And folks with 401(k) plans started switching their holdings into large-cap tech.

Can you guess what happened? Well, around spring of 2000, tech took a bad tumble. Intel, Cisco, Dell Computer, Sun Microsystems, Microsoft—all good companies and all tremendous players over the prior three or more years—got creamed. The tech-heavy NASDAQ index fell almost 40 percent in the calendar year 2000 and almost 80 percent from its March, 2000 high to its 2002 low.

In truth, the year 2000 was not a good one for stocks in general. But if you were in a value fund that had transformed itself into a tech-growth fund, you were really in trouble. Growth went south in a big way, but value more or less held its own and some types of value funds—small-cap, for example—were up significantly. So if you thought you were in value but really were in growth, you got the worst of both worlds: What you thought you were in stayed even or went up but what you were really in fell like a rock. *Surprise!*

So it's important for managers to be style-specific and to have style discipline. I like to see investors use an investment advisory team with multiple managers, each operating in a different style. As long as the managers aren't buying the same stocks and stick with their disciplines and are measured against reliable benchmarks, then you can get an accurate reading as to how they're performing.

Judging performance, again, takes a seasoned eye. For example, if your portfolio grew by 28 percent in a year, that would sound pretty good, right? Generally, yes. But a few years ago, a large growth portfolio should have brought in about 38 percent and a 28 percent return would have been underperforming. By contrast, a large-value portfolio that did 12 percent that year when the S&P did 28 percent might look anemic. But actually, 12 percent might have put you 20 percent to 30 percent above what other large-value managers were earning. So it's critical to understand which benchmark you're using as an evaluation tool. And then you and your advisor can hold your money managers to that mark.

What Does Your Pie Chart Look Like?

Your financial advisor will help you figure out what mix of funds is right for your Bucket No. 3. Your risk tolerance, how you feel about the market's future, and other factors are taken into account. A classic, all-growth portfolio might look like Figure 7.1. What

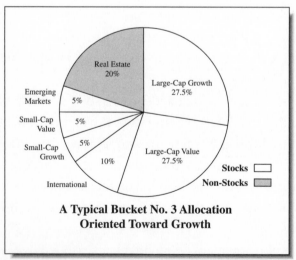

A Typical Bucket No. 3 Allocation
Oriented Toward Growth

Figure 7.1

the advisor will try to do is to find asset classes that don't move in lockstep with one another. For example, tech stocks (which are generally in the large-growth category) might have been down almost 40 percent in the year 2000, but the average growth mutual fund was down only about 6 percent. So even though they both were down, the combination of the two still would have given you a much better portfolio than if you had just one.

Lump-Sum Investing or Dollar-Cost Averaging?

You read a lot in the popular financial press about the joys of dollar-cost averaging (DCA). That's where money is invested in increments over a long period rather than as a lump sum. There are times when DCA makes perfect sense. When you're automatically putting a part of your paycheck into your 401(k) plan at work or adding to your IRA, you are dollar-cost averaging. And that's fine. But usually that's not the way to invest your Bucket No. 3. For me, using DCA for that task is too much like trying to time the market, and you know what I think about that. In fact, consider this . . .

LUCIA'S LAW 24

Dollar-cost averaging is like a little voice saying, "I'm so afraid of this market that I'll just invest in dribs and drabs." Long-term investors needn't have that fear.

The average bull market runs almost 40 months, and the average bear market about 19 months. Thus, roughly every third or fourth year, stocks have a down year. But that means three out of four are up years. If you dollar-cost average in an up market, you're going to have a lot of money sitting on the sidelines before you're fully invested. So you're going to miss out on a lot of potential return, and to me that's foolish.

What I recommend instead is a *Buckets of Money* strategy and broad asset allocation for the stock portfolio in Bucket No. 3. Don't try to pick a good time to jump into the market or try to invest a little bit in both good times and bad. Instead, asset allocation means using your head (and your advisor's know-how) to set up the best possible model—and then allow this diversification to smooth out the market's ride as much as possible.

I repeat: There are *no* guarantees. But if you have a multi-asset, multi-style, multi-manager approach, there's not a whole lot that can upset your apple cart over the long run. If the market goes up, you're going to go up. If the market goes down, you're going to go down—but you're not going to get walloped the way someone will who tried and failed to time the market. Also, remember that in a down stock market your *Buckets* strategy will include bonds, cash, and real estate that will likely move in a more positive direction.

Judging Performance

How do you and your advisor decide if a manager is doing a good job? The truth is, the markets continually fluctuate, sectors soar and fall, and styles of investing ebb and flow. You don't want to cut somebody off at the knees because, say, he or she is a large-tech fund manager and the year 2000 was a lousy one for large-tech stocks. Or even if large-tech had an okay year but this particular manager did not. But if he or she *consistently* fails to meet benchmarks, then this manager has to go.

You're going to need some help in figuring out if the fund managers are performing well. Are they running the fund according to its stated objectives and not chasing after the latest hot equities?

Are they meeting their benchmarks, which usually means one of the accepted indexes, such as the Dow Jones (for big firms), the Russell 2000 (for small-cap stocks), and the Standard & Poor's 500 or the Wilshire 5000 (for the broad market).

In addition, if yours is a taxable portfolio, is the manager doing the best for you tax-wise? If not, you're giving up real money, real rate of return, that you don't need to.

I'll talk some more about some of these issues in the next chapter, but the point is that everybody's situation is unique. To make the very best use of your Bucket No 3, you're going to need help. And to coin a phrase, you get what you pay for. If you hire a really sharp and talented financial advisor who understands the architecture of your financial plan, that will compensate for a lot of things, even underperformance. For instance, if one portfolio produces a 10 percent return but gives back 2.5 percent in taxes while another, more tax-efficient fund produces a 9 percent net return, which would you prefer?

Kinds of Stock Investments

Even if you have a good advisor, you still will want to become a knowledgeable investor. This way you can understand something about the markets and can have a dialogue with your team: this means regular meetings with your advisor and occasional meetings with individual money managers, or other experts, as needed. Let's look at some of these vehicles and how they might help or hinder your Bucket No. 3.

Balanced Funds

Most mutual funds invest in just one asset class, say, stocks. But a balanced fund puts a portion of its assets into each of the four major asset classes: stocks, bonds, government securities, and cash. It sounds good in theory—like instant diversification. But to me they're akin to market-timing funds. The idea is that the manager will bulk up on bonds or stocks, depending on where he or she thinks the market is going. But, in truth, nobody knows. Even if you're the smartest person in America, you don't know what the market is going to do. So it's much better to design a good diversified model than try to predict highs and lows.

Growth and Income Funds

Similarly, these funds split the assets between stocks and bonds. But the problem is much the same as with the balanced fund— the manager is tempted to bet on which sector is likely to be on the rise. However, some growth and income funds invest largely in income-producing stocks that pay dividends. These may be quite adequate for the value portion of the portfolio.

Sector Funds

These funds buy stocks of only one industry—energy, telecommunications, airlines, retailers, or just about any field you can think of. But such sectors can ricochet wildly, so these are very speculative. Sector funds should be an option only if an investor has money to burn and wants to play the market with a small amount of his portfolio, say 5 percent. If you're hooked on daring challenges and can afford to lose the money, go right ahead. But it's a gamble, like putting 5 percent in gold. Most of us are better off allowing a professional money manager make the decisions on which sectors to include, for instance, in a large-cap growth fund. Something quite interesting happens when you combine a group of sector funds—say, 5 percent in telecom, 5 percent in health care, 5 percent in financial services, and 5 percent in natural resources. Together, they may make up a large-cap growth fund on steroids. But this type of strategy is not for the fainthearted and needs the careful attention of a qualified advisor.

Index Funds

These funds attempt to duplicate the performance of a market index by buying the same stocks that compose the index, whether it be, for example, the Dow Jones Industrial Average, the NASDAQ Composite, the NASDAQ 100, or the Standard & Poor's 500. These could make a lot of sense for the Bucket No. 3 investor, especially in a taxable account.

Index funds are effectively unmanaged funds because the fund buys the stocks in a particular index and then just holds them. Since most indexes are market-capitalization weighted, most of your money goes into the largest 50 companies of, say, the S&P 500. Thus, when the market is going down, you're investing more money in those big companies. Likewise, when the market is soaring, you are placing your money in the most expensive stocks. Among the advantages of index funds are that they have low turnover and thus are fairly tax-efficient.

In recent years, some managers who actively traded have had trouble beating the indexes. The S&P 500, for example, is mostly weighted toward growth stocks. Thus, value managers are not going to beat that index when growth stocks are hot as they were in the late 1990s. So I sometimes recommend index funds for efficient markets like the Dow, S&P, and to a much lesser extent, NASDAQ. But for investing in less efficient markets like international stocks, small caps, emerging markets, and the like, I think you'd be better off to have a money manager picking the stocks and being geared to pulling the trigger when and if the trigger needs to be pulled. That may well be the best of all worlds—to have your portfolio partially managed and partially indexed.

You can also use active management for the less efficient markets like small caps and international funds where stock picking is paramount and use indexing for the more efficient markets like large-growth and value. That way, when indexing is in favor and momentum is driving the market up, you have the advantage. And when active managers are in the driver's seat, you're still okay.

Exchange-Traded Funds

You can also buy certain stocks that track the performance of an index. These are called *exchange-traded funds,* or ETFs. They trade just like any other stock but will perform very near the index they track. You can buy these stocks, unlike mutual funds, throughout the trading day rather than getting the price at the close of the trading session. So more active traders prefer ETFs over funds. Frankly, I don't care one way or the other because I'm not an advocate of active trading. ETFs are usually cheaper than index funds if you are not constantly adding new money through dollar-cost averaging. Otherwise, buying an index fund will work just fine.

Just a few, quick words on some other types of stock funds:

- *Large-capitalization funds (or Large Caps).* These funds buy stocks of big companies worth a lot of money. General Electric and General Motors, for example, are unlikely to go broke. Thus, these funds are safer than some, though their size also makes them less likely to spurt upward.
- *Small-cap funds.* You guessed it! These are funds of smaller companies that have a greater risk of going belly-up but also more potential for quantum increases in profit.

- *Equity income funds.* These, also known as dividend yield funds, buy stocks that pay dividends, meaning usually larger, established companies. These funds have become a little more popular because of the new 15 percent maximum capital gains tax on dividends.
- *Global funds.* These funds buy stocks from nations around the globe, including the United States.
- *International funds.* These funds buy international stocks but exclude any U.S. stocks, thus helping you to diversify if you already own funds holding American companies.

There are many more kinds of stock mutual funds. But those are some of the obvious categories you may run into when huddling with your financial advisor. One other distinction you might want to be alert to is the difference between *open-end* and *closed-end* funds. Most funds are open-end, meaning they offer an unlimited number of shares forever and thus you can sell back your shares (known as *redeeming* them) to the mutual fund company when you want to take your money out.

By contrast, a closed-end fund sells only a certain number of shares. When you want to sell, you can't redeem them with the company and instead must find buyers on the New York Stock Exchange. Thus, the sale price isn't the NAV but whatever you can negotiate, which usually means something less than the NAV. A buyer may think he or she is getting them cheaply, but in truth closed-end shares hardly ever rise to their NAV, so they're not likely to be much of a bargain. Every so often a closed-end fund sells at a substantial discount to its NAV, and there may be some good money to be made, but that's usually not the case. The bottom line is that closed-end equity funds are widely misunderstood, so I don't do much with them. You probably shouldn't, either.

What About Families of Funds?

Many large mutual fund companies have dozens or scores of funds covering every aspect of the market—growth, value, different sectors, big-cap, small-cap, you name it. Which raises the question: Is there an advantage to keeping your funds within one fund family? The definitive answer: Yes and no.

At some fund families, they manage by committee. That is, all the managers share their favorite stocks, then go out and buy roughly the same stocks for their portfolios. That defeats the purpose of diversification. When the market tide eventually turns against them (*and it will!*), they'll all need to sell. That means an awful lot of money will leave the family. Which, in turn, means more selling, which means yet more capital gains and higher taxes for you—and even worse, the possibility of lower returns.

For a small investor, sticking with one family may be a good idea. Especially if you paid a load. But for any *Bucketeer* with a hefty sum to put in Bucket No. 3, the smart course would be to work with your advisor to find either a family that doesn't have a lot of overlap among its funds' holdings, or choose nonoverlapping funds from various families.

The Alpha Variant

One strategy I really like for Bucket No. 3 involves combining the stock-picking ability of top money managers with a diversified indexing approach. Why? Because active management beats indexing some of the time, and indexing beats active management some of the time. So this is sort of a have-your-cake-and-eat-it-too approach. You get the consistent performance of an index fund with the possibility of a high alpha performance (that is, one that exceeds the benchmark).

To do this you need to (1) hire an oversight manager, (2) design an asset-allocation model, and (3) instruct the manager to invest half your Bucket No. 3 money into a concentrated portfolio of mutual funds he or she selects and the other half into index funds or exchange-traded funds. This last move helps to broaden the risk and lower costs.

As for the allocation model, because this is Bucket No. 3, you'll want all growth (no bonds here). But you will need to decide whether you want to diversify globally or just invest in domestic companies. There are firms—such as Morningstar Investment Services, among others—that for a fee will select and monitor money managers for the active half of your Bucket No. 3 portfolio. He or she will use technology as well as personal savvy to create a diversified portfolio of about eight funds. Then the manager duplicates that same portfolio using index funds or ETFs that will mirror the performance of the market itself. The cost? Probably in the 1 percent to 2 percent range.

While this active, alpha manager strives for overperformance, the index portfolio provides stability. Some would argue that this is a fence-sitting posture, neither wholly timid nor wholly bold. But I would rather be 50 percent right than 100 percent wrong.

The Joys of Rebalancing

The typical Bucket No. 3 investor doesn't need to worry about switching funds as much as he or she does about rebalancing. If your fund managers are meeting their benchmarks, you don't need to worry about changing funds. But you do need to think about rebalancing.

You may remember from the early chapters that rebalancing is when you periodically redistribute your money to keep consistent with your goals. This is especially important when markets fluctuate a lot as they did in the year 2000. Let's say you were supposed to have 30 percent of your portfolio invested in large growth. But large growth got killed in 2000, so your overall portfolio fell 8 percent, and 6 percent of that was attributable to the decline in large growth.

You look at your portfolio and see that your large growth has declined from 30 percent to 27 percent of the total. So you're underweighted there and overweighted in other categories. What do you do? You buy growth. You take some money from the categories that have done well, and you plop it into growth. It's sort of like being on a hot streak in Las Vegas. Do you take your winnings and bet them all on the next roll of the dice or spin of the wheel? You *could* (and casino owners love those who do). But a more prudent idea is to stick some of your gain into your pocket to fund next summer's vacation or make the next car payment.

That takes discipline. But in investing, discipline works. Rebalancing is far better than market timing because over the long haul you're forcing yourself to sell high and buy low. You sell the good stuff and buy the ugly stuff, and it usually pays off. True to form, stocks seemingly bottomed out in October 2002. Meanwhile, bonds and real estate had been on a tear. A reassessment of your portfolio back to its proper mix would have caused you to sell the bonds and buy stocks. Through August 2003 the S&P 500 posted a 30 percent increase since the October low while bonds in July 2003 suffered one of the worse sell-offs in many years. So rebalancing really can work!

Helping you rebalance is another task your advisor gets paid to do. You will need to set the criteria, such as how often (monthly, quarterly, or yearly) and how much of a differential will trigger a rebalancing (for example, when your percentages are off by 2 percent or by 3 percent). Further, you'll need to give him or her guidelines as to whether to rebalance just retirement accounts (in which taxes on sales are deferred) or all accounts and how much cost is acceptable to execute this buying and selling.

Investment Fads to Avoid

Whatever you do, avoid fad investing. Among the dubious, fad-like ideas are:

Dogs of the Dow

This is a concept in which investors buy the poorest performing of the Dow Jones Industrial Average stocks each year. It's based on the idea that stocks with the highest dividend yields are most likely to rise in price. That's a great idea when it works and a bad idea when it doesn't.

When value stocks are in favor, the Dogs may be excellent performers. But as a long-term investing philosophy, forget about the Dogs of the Dow. Ditto for several variations, such as the Small Dogs theory, in which you invest in, say, the five lowest-priced of the 10 highest-yielding Dow stocks.

Remember, there's a reason they're called Dogs. The reality is if you want some high-yielding stocks as *part* of your total asset allocation, that's fine. But if you want them as your total asset allocation, that's foolish.

Direct Reinvestment Plans

DRIPs are one of those concepts that sounds good on the surface because it allows the small investor to avoid brokerage commissions and buy fractional shares (at a discount in some cases) while dollar-cost averaging. But in truth, it's a nightmare of accounting. Tax-wise, DRIPs are so complicated you practically need to hire a Big 4 accounting firm to figure out the cost basis of your shares. I think DRIPs in a personal account are a waste of time. If you must buy DRIPs, please do so in your IRA.

In my opinion, the rise and sophistication of mutual funds has made DRIPs an idea whose time has come *and* gone. If you can buy a mutual fund for $25 a month and in so doing get diversification, professional management, and precise tax accounting, why would you want to bother with DRIPS? Beats me.

Buying on Splits

What's better, two nickels or a dime? That's the question at the heart of buying on splits. The answer, of course, is: It doesn't matter. A split occurs when a company's board of directors changes (usually increases) the number of outstanding shares. If you had 100 shares and the stock split 2-for-1, you'd have 200 shares, but each would be worth only half as much and pay half the dividends. So what have you gained?

And in some cases, buying on the split can be disastrous. The stock of wireless leader Qualcomm, for example, grew at a mind-boggling 2,400 percent in 1999, making it the biggest gainer on the NASDAQ. It split 4-for-1 at year's end, and although a PaineWebber analyst had predicted it would hit $1,000 a presplit share ($250 after the split), it succumbed in the ensuing tech wreck and most recently has been trading in the $30s.

It's true that firms that split tend to be confident about their future and thus, their stock may be on the rise. But if the company and the public like the stock so much, it's probably going to be on the rise whether there's a split or not, and the spurt in price that sometimes follows a stock-split announcement may be temporary. Instead of watching splits, watch the company's fundamentals. If you're investing for the long term, you want a firm that has strong enough revenue, earnings, and dividend growth to keep on track, with or without a split.

Rolling Stocks and Other Strategies

This involves figuring out which stocks move in a predictable pattern, then buying at the low end of the range and selling at the high end—and doing it over and over again. The trouble, of course, lies with the word *predictable.* The bear market of 2000 pretty much killed all of the rolling stock investors, market timers, day traders, fad investors, and the like. These are short-term strategies that may work for a while on some stocks. But sooner or later either that stock or the market as a whole will throw you a curve. Again, it's better to invest for the long term and in companies with real potential rather than those that may or may not be predictably cyclical.

Nonstock Holdings for Bucket No. 3

Real Estate

Stocks should be the primary vehicle in your Bucket No. 3. But there may be room for other long-term investments as well, principally real estate. In fact, I'd recommend a real estate allocation of 10 percent to 20 percent in your Bucket No. 3.

Like stocks, real estate over the long term can grow in value and produce income. And it's usually not as volatile as stocks because it takes a lot longer to buy or sell than just calling up your mutual fund company or financial advisor. So there's less day-to-day fluctuation in prices, and that's good. But on the other hand, this lack of liquidity also means you can get stuck with an unsalable piece of property on which you're paying a mortgage, taxes, and upkeep, and that's not so great. So real estate, while worth considering for Bucket No. 3, brings its own baggage. I think real estate is better as a Bucket No. 3 complement to stocks rather than as a replacement for stocks. In the next chapter, I'll talk about some situations where real estate might be a good way to go. Of course, there are different ways to own real estate. Let's look at some possibilities.

Income Property

Keep in mind that buying rental property usually requires a large initial cash outlay as well as lots of management hassles for you, the landlord. Ideally, if you go the real estate route for Bucket No. 3, you ought to be diversified there, too, meaning multiple properties—and that can really get costly.

Owner-Occupied Real Estate

Most people already have a fair amount of real estate if one considers the family home. Is that a Bucket No. 3 investment? It *could* be, but probably you shouldn't look at it that way. After all, unlike your stocks and income property, you can't exactly sell it and live off it in retirement—you'll still need a place to live. So the fact that your home appreciated may not mean too much if when you sell it, you have to buy another, equally expensive home.

If the value of your home rises significantly and there's a way to tap into that equity by selling and thus help fund your retirement, great! This works well when you sell a really expensive home and move to an area where houses are cheaper. Since married couples can exclude up to $500,000 of capital gains on their principal residence (up to $250,000 for single people), this could be a nifty way to get extra income at retirement. But it's best not to count on your home as part of your Bucket No. 3. In fact, this extra equity is more like a Bucket No. 1 or 2 when you ultimately sell—a great place to find some cash for immediate or deferred income.

If your home turns out to be a great investment, that's a bonus. But if it doesn't, you've still planned well and will be okay. And, understand, the house may not work out as an investment because (1) it may not rise in value, (2) it may rise but you may not be able to sell it for what it's worth when you want to, and (3) you may need to buy another one, which could end up costing you as much or more. The best plan, then, is to just live in your house and enjoy it. If it turns out to help your retirement, that's a windfall-but not something you're counting on.

Limited Partnerships

There are limited partnerships (LPs) for oil and gas exploration, motion pictures, and even Broadway plays, as well as for real estate. These were big a decade or so ago, although changes in tax laws have reduced their allure somewhat. The basic idea is that instead of buying property on your own, you pool your funds with other investors (the limited partners) and give the money to a manager (the general partner) who buys, operates, and eventually sells the property at a profit, which is then split proportionally among the investors.

Such partnerships got a bad name in the 1980s because some general partners took advantage of the investors. But if you've got a trustworthy general partner and if there are strong economics to the deal (as opposed to just the lure of tax write-offs), it makes some sense for small investors to join forces to buy larger and potentially more profitable pieces of property than they could afford individually. Going in with 30 other investors to buy a $3 million apartment house, say, can be much better for your Bucket No. 3 than buying a $300,000 duplex and having to personally manage it.

But be careful! The potential for abuse always exists because the limited partner has no way of controlling what goes on at the general-partner level until it's too late. Then the only option is to sue, and that's a losing game for the investor. Remember the general partner has all of the control and the limited partner has virtually none—so know the general partner well, or don't do it at all.

Real Estate Investment Trusts

Real estate investment trusts (REITs) are firms whose primary business is owning and managing real estate properties such as office buildings, apartment complexes, hotels, warehouses, health care facilities, shopping malls, or golf courses. Individual REITs (pronounced "reets") may focus on just one of these sectors. A REIT's goal is to generate income from the rent paid by tenants or lessees. It can also produce gains when a property it owns is sold at a profit.

To qualify as a REIT and thus avoid paying corporate taxes, a REIT must have at least 100 investors and agree to pass 90 percent of all its taxable income to its shareholders each year. The taxable income REITs earn and pass through to their investors is at the top of the corporate food chain. By that I mean that corporations are obligated to pay operating expenses, such as rent, first before making interest payments to bondholders or dividends to stockholders. Thus, if a firm hits a financial rough spot, the rent it pays to the REIT management company gets top priority.

REITs are somewhat akin to partnerships, except their shares usually trade on the stock exchanges. Most REIT investors, unlike those in limited partnerships, can sell whenever they wish. So this is a very liquid kind of real estate investment. Unlike limited partnerships, REITs are public companies with independent boards and must comply with all of the same SEC filings as other public companies. Thus, they're better regulated than limited partnerships.

But the fact that REIT shares can be traded is both good news and bad. REIT shares wax and wane, just like any other stock. So buying REITs does give you real estate and may produce a fine income stream, but it doesn't shield you from the market's volatility.

That's why I prefer nontraded REITs. These are REITs in the growth stage, still raising money from investors to purchase commercial buildings, hotels, assisted-living facilities, and the like. Because they're not being traded, their prices don't fluctuate daily. They are usually private en route to becoming a listed, or public, company. So they are a little less liquid but they are a good complement for Bucket No. 3's stock allocation: less volatile than stocks but with returns similar to that of the stock market.

REITs do provide excellent diversification in a Bucket No. 3 portfolio. Studies show a 20 percent equity REIT allocation in a balanced portfolio increased the return over time and decreased the volatility. That's because REITs do not correlate perfectly with stocks or bonds, and that's a good thing. You don't want asset classes that all move together at the same time. Over the past decade or so, REITs have moved in the opposite direction of stocks and bonds about 75 percent of the time. That's good diversification.

There are many different types of REITs, such as those that hold residential, commercial, or health care properties. Each requires due diligence before investing, but they may be suitable as part of Bucket No. 3 while at the same time producing income to reduce the amount of capital needed to invest in Bucket No. 1. Particularly desirable are low-leveraged REITs, that is, those without a lot of debt because they own most of their properties free and clear. That way even if the real estate market struggles and occupancy rates decline, it's unlikely there would be a total loss as can occur if you own the stock of a firm that goes bankrupt. A low-leveraged REIT in difficult times may have to cut its dividend, but it's not likely you will lose your principal sum.

Variable Universal Life, or the Legacy Bucket

Life insurance is not primarily intended to be a Bucket No. 3 investment. And it's true that insurance and insurance salespeople sometimes are unpopular. But many times a variable universal life (VUL) policy is the best investment for those not needing to spend all of the money in Bucket No. 3 and wanting to pass on the highest after-tax inheritance. In certain cases, a properly funded VUL policy can be a great tax break and supplement your 401(k), Roth IRA, 529 plan, and Education IRA by producing tax-favored income at retirement when you may need it the most.

That's why I recommend it—for some people—as a "Legacy Bucket," a sort of sub-bucket of Bucket No. 3. Where else can you get your money to grow tax-free, choose to invest among a large selection of mutual fund–like accounts (known as *subaccounts*), and then when it comes time to take the money out, make tax-free withdrawals of your cost basis and borrow your gain tax-free? Plus, when you die, the death benefit pays off all of the loans, and the balance is paid to your heirs tax-free.

This isn't for people with low or modest cash flow and a need for temporary coverage. They should buy term life insurance, not as an investment but as protection against financial loss, such as happens when the breadwinner dies. But VUL is definitely worth looking into for those with higher incomes, more significant cash flows, and a mindset for long-term investing. If you either can't qualify for Roth IRAs because your income is too high, or if you're already funding your Roth, SEP, Keogh, 401(k), or other retirement plan to the max, VUL might be worth considering. (Because variable universal has elements of both life insurance and a securities contract, the policies are regulated under federal securities laws and must be sold with a prospectus. There is a risk of loss, including principal.)

If you bought a VUL policy and funded it with the same amount as you would put in mutual funds over a long period of time, you'd likely get a similar income stream, but it would be tax-free. In addition, you'd be insured every year for the rest of your life, and your family would get the tax-free death benefit upon your death.

You can make the most of the tax advantages if you fund the variable universal policy liberally in its early years so there's adequate value accumulated later when you want to access funds. But once you've built up accumulated value, you can take money out tax-free by loans or withdrawals. Or, if you have already retired or soon will be, a low-load variable universal life policy can also be a great help in giving you the kind of income you need to live out your years and/or providing a lump-sum benefit to your heirs or favorite charity when you die.

In either case, funding your Bucket No. 3 in part with a cash-value insurance policy can be a low-cost way to:

- Provide a potential return similar to mutual funds after taxes
- Supplement your retirement income tax-free
- Restore or increase the purchasing power of your *Buckets* by providing growth in excess of the rate of inflation
- Preserve your net worth so that when you die, it can be passed along to heirs or charities

In fact, no other investment vehicle seems to offer, all in one package, the potential for tax-deferred growth, tax-free transfers among portfolios, tax-advantaged access to cash accumulation, and generally income tax–free capital transfer at death.

But I repeat, this is *not* a short-term investment. Many of the tax advantages disappear if the premiums paid in the first 15 years exceed IRS restrictions, or if you withdraw too much too early. It's also important that you consider your ability to fund the policy through cycles. As with any investment, regular monitoring of your results is recommended. Of course, the returns from the mutual fund–like subaccounts are not guaranteed, and there are insurance charges for the insurance protection.

Further, once you're withdrawing money from the policy, you've got to leave enough in to cover the death benefit. Otherwise, the policy lapses. If the policy does lapse or is surrendered, any amount borrowed above your cost basis will be taxed as ordinary income.

Taking money out permanently reduces the death benefit. Therefore, any withdrawals or loans are best taken when tax-free income and a reduction in the death benefit are part of an overall strategy—for instance, if your children are grown and no longer dependent on you. If this has appeal for you, you might want to check out low-load VUL offerings and see if a Legacy Bucket would help you.

Other Nonstock, Non–Real Estate Investments

Some folks like to go beyond stocks and real estate in search of other long-term assets that *may* appreciate in their Bucket No. 3. I'm dubious. Too often this means they invest in something they really like, such as old movie posters or Cabbage Patch dolls.

And it's fine that they enjoy those, and even better if the items increase in value over the years. But an investor's fondness for the objects can obscure reason and good judgment. Besides, stocks or real estate have proven track records as growth vehicles. So they are much safer places to put your retirement savings.

Collectibles

This means things like coins, gems, stamps, art, antiques, vintage wines, or comic books. The value of these ebb and flow in public favor. I don't like them as investments. I think collectibles are a hobby, not a true investment, and lack any semblance of predictability. At least with stocks, you know what the long-term trend is. I don't think there is any predictable trend with old cars or diamonds or baseball cards. If you really like old cars, diamonds, or baseball cards, great. Collect as many as you can afford, display them nicely, admire them lovingly, and show them off to friends and family. And if they appreciate, you're ahead of the game. Just don't count on that appreciation—and don't consider it part of your *Buckets*.

Precious Metals

Every investment text ever written says that gold is a good inflation hedge. But we haven't had serious inflation in quite a while, and anybody who bought gold in the last 10 to 15 years has been sorely disappointed. With rare exceptions, precious metals have been flat, or worse, since the late 1970s, and my advice is to ignore the advice of the occasional doomsayer who tells you that gold and silver will save you in the event of a worldwide economic cataclysm. A precious metal investment is a market-timing decision, and you know by now how I feel about timing the market!

There is more that could be said about what to put in Bucket No. 3. And I'll give you some more examples in the next chapter. But for now, keep in mind that:

- *You need to reserve Bucket No. 3 for long-term potential growth.* You almost never put money market funds or bonds in this *Bucket.* Your best bet is stock mutual funds and some real estate, preferably nontraded REITs.
- *You will need a financial advisor.* He or she will help you get properly diversified and keep tabs on the fund managers so that they stick to their objectives and meet their benchmarks.
- *You must rebalance your portfolio periodically.* Your advisor can do this, but you can and should set the criteria.

PART IV

BUCKETIZING YOUR LIFE

CHAPTER 8

Getting Your *Buckets* All Lined Up

Now that you know what kinds of investments work best for each *Bucket*, what do you do? How do you organize your *Buckets* and when, if ever, do you change that setup?

One of the beauties of the *Buckets* strategy is that it's so flexible. I've often mentioned the example of the three main *Buckets* and time frames of 7, 7, and 14 years, respectively. But, as I mentioned, there's nothing cut in bronze about that. You might want to do longer or shorter *Buckets* or even, in effect, change the number of *Buckets*. As you'll see in this chapter, it's quite possible and/or desirable—depending on individual circumstances—to vary the number of years or to make *Buckets* within the *Buckets*.

What's most important is that you have a personal investment strategy built around *you*—your goals, your time frame, and your tolerance for risk. In today's complex investment world, even expert investors find it hard to create and implement a well-structured investment plan on their own. So, again, I strongly urge you to work with investment professionals who understand your needs and can help you develop a prudent strategy that will both protect and grow your wealth.

So you can better work with those professionals, let's look at some of the scenarios and principles you might encounter whether you are (1) a long way from retirement, (2) nearing retirement, or (3) already retired.

Preretirement

If you're well shy of retirement, you're in an enviable position. You've got many years, perhaps decades, to let your wealth grow. You can afford to take more risks than someone who's approaching retirement or is already there.

All your retirement plan money is going to be in Bucket No. 2 or Bucket No. 3. If you're, say, 30 years old and have a secure, well-paying job, you theoretically could put all your retirement assets in your Bucket No. 3—in other words, you *could* load up on stocks and real estate and let them appreciate.

But I don't recommend that even for a carefree 30-year-old. A better plan would be to put 20 percent of your retirement assets in, say, tax-free municipal bonds in Bucket No. 2 and the remaining 80 percent in the Bucket No. 3 stocks and real estate. Then you wouldn't lose all that much return in exchange for much less volatility. Also, if the stock market were to go into steep decline, you might want to tap into Bucket No. 2 to take advantage of the next bounce. You couldn't do that if you didn't have at least some safe money on the sidelines.

If you are working now, you're probably putting money into a 401(k), an IRA, a Roth IRA, a SEP, or some other retirement plan. (If you aren't, you *should* be.) If retirement is still 10 or 15 years off, your asset-allocation model might feature an over-weight Bucket No. 3, an underweight Bucket No. 2, and perhaps nothing in Bucket No. 1 because you don't need an income apart from your salary. The amount of time you leave your money in Bucket No. 2 and Bucket No. 3 could be longer or shorter than in our example, depending on when you want to retire. Although you may not yet need income, you *will* need safety. So as you get closer and closer to retirement, you probably will want to swell your Bucket No. 2 to make sure you have a certain amount of safe money.

There's a real danger in not doing so. For instance, imagine somebody who retired in the year 2000 and had most of his or her retirement money in Bucket No. 3 and most of that tied up in tech stocks. (That wouldn't happen if you adhere to our asset-allocation model. But, hey, there are always those mavericks who don't follow instructions!) Even the best such tech stocks—for instance, Intel, Cisco, and Sun Microsystems—took a terrific hit in 2000 and beyond. Those are arguably great companies, but it may take several years for relatively new owners of those stocks to get their money back. And with some tech stocks, they may never get back to even.

Thus, a tech stock–heavy retirement portfolio would have been a disaster if the year 2000—or shortly thereafter—was when you were going to need the dough. In fact, I have fielded scores of telephone calls on my radio talk show from individuals retired or nearing retirement who were overweighted in tech stocks and are now forced into either postponing retirement, going back to work, or acquiring a taste for dog food.

So, please, don't look for the quick buck, the fast turnaround. In fact, if you're going to buy stocks, even good ones, you'd better plan on owning them for, say, 10 to 15 years or more. Only that way may the market risks diminish to something manageable.

Nearing Retirement

Planning gets a bit more critical as you approach retirement. One of the key questions: *What to do about Social Security?*

If you start drawing your Social Security check, your need for income from Bucket No. 1 and Bucket No. 2 likely will fall. So you might be able to divert some of your Bucket No. 1 funds to Bucket No. 2 or Bucket No. 3. You also might be able to lengthen the amount of time you leave money in Bucket No. 3. (Remember, the longer you leave it in, the more likely it'll grow and the less risk you face of losing money.)

When should you start drawing down your Social Security account? You can draw a partial benefit at age 62. That amounts to about 80 percent of the fuller benefit you'd receive if you wait until the normal retirement age of 65 to 67.

Does it make sense to get the benefit as soon as possible? Generally, yes. The IRS used to penalize those who worked after age 65, or their normal retirement date. But new rules generally allow working seniors to collect full Social Security benefits. However, those under their normal retirement age of 65 to 67 will have to give back some of their Social Security benefits if they earn more than about $12,000 a year. So taking your Social Security at age 62 may not be advisable if you continue to work. New IRS rules also have lengthened life-expectancy schedules, thus reducing the post-age-70½ required minimum distribution for those with tax-deferred retirement plans. That means retirees can let more of their IRA nest eggs grow tax-deferred for a longer time.

As your retirement nears, you'll want to begin deemphasizing Bucket No. 3. In short, you're going to want more income and less risk exposure to stocks.

Upon Retirement

Once you retire, you probably will want to siphon money out of Bucket No. 3 and feed Bucket No. 1 and Bucket No. 2. But keep in mind that no matter if you're a retiree or a pre-retiree, your individual circumstance may dictate changes to our model. For example, your estate plan might suggest how your money is invested. If you had, say, a $75,000 pension from your former employer, you might not need a Bucket No. 1 at all. Or maybe not even a Bucket No. 2. You might just live off the pension and put all *Buckets* money into a Bucket No. 3 that would be strictly for your kids' or your grandkids' inheritance.

How you invested that Bucket No. 3 might be influenced by taxability. For instance, you might want all stocks in your personal account invested in Bucket No. 3 while your REIT investment in Bucket No. 3 is funded with IRA money. That way you get a more favorable 15 percent maximum tax on the dividend and long-term capital gains if you want to get your hands on the money before you die. And then after you're gone, the kids inherit the gains free of income tax.

Assets that spin off taxable income, such as REITs, growth-and-income funds, and high-turnover mutual funds, are better held in IRAs. That way you don't need to worry about taxation because an IRA is already tax-deferred until the money is withdrawn. Any other Bucket No. 3 money outside your IRA and in your personal account could contain individual stocks, tax-managed mutual funds, or index funds because these are usually low-turnover funds and fairly tax-efficient.

Thus, you hold the types of assets more likely to produce an ordinary income tax hit in your IRA and those with the potential to receive stock dividends and long-term capital gains tax treatment in your personal account. With ordinary-income rates in the high 30 percent range (plus possible state income taxes) and capital gains rates as low as 5 percent (or even 0 percent in some cases) and as high as 15 percent, divvying up your *Buckets* in a tax-efficient manner is very important.

The Joys of Tax Management

As you can see, everybody's situation is going to be different. For one person an annuity may be a great idea, and for another it may be terrible. The same holds true for municipal bonds, real estate, or any other kind of investment. All of which leads us to some advanced *Bucketeering*, the motto of which might be . . .

LUCIA'S LAW 25

The easiest way to make money is to stop losing it.

Many times, with proper planning, you can stay in a lower tax bracket. For example, let's say you and your spouse have a $1 million portfolio spread among CDs ($300,000), government bonds ($300,000), and retail mutual funds ($400,000) that are not tax-efficient. In other words, you are getting creamed each year with Form 1099s for short-term capital gains and dividends. Further, let's say the CDs earn 6 percent (about $18,000 a year), the bonds 7 percent ($21,000), and the funds produce income of about $20,000 from dividends and short-term capital gains.

That's ordinary income from your investments of approximately $51,000 and dividend income of about $8,000. Add to that, say, a $30,000 pension, and you're looking at a taxable income of $89,000—which would put you firmly in the 25 percent federal marginal tax bracket. (I live in California, so if this were me, I'd have to add a 9.3 percent marginal state tax bracket, too.)

However, with just a few changes, you could get a radically different result. For example, you could switch from government bonds to tax-free bonds. That would reduce taxes on your bonds to nothing. Further, you could put the CDs into a tax-deferred annuity, or if you need income, into an immediate annuity, which would reduce taxable income there to around $5,000. And you could tax-manage the mutual funds and maybe get that taxable income down to about $8,000 or less. Now your investment income is $13,000. Add that to your pension, and you get a gross taxable income of $43,000. *Voila!* Now you're in the 15 percent marginal tax bracket.

Instead of paying 25 percent in taxes on a portion of your income, you now owe 15 percent on that portion. That's a big difference. Or, to put it another way, you're earning an additional 10 percent and all you did was tax-manage your accounts. The point is: You can legally manipulate your tax situation considerably by just using various tax-favored investment vehicles and some fairly sophisticated tax-management techniques. A good financial advisor can help greatly in this area.

How you structure your ordinary income versus long-term capital gains can be crucial. If, say, 50 percent of your portfolio is taxed now as ordinary income, that means the other 50 percent will be taxed at the long-term capital gains rate. If you can tax-manage your portfolio so as to decrease to 10 percent or 20 percent the portion that's taxed as ordinary income, then 80 percent or 90 percent will be taxed at the lower, long-term capital gains rate. That's a pretty good return, and you haven't added any money, just divvied it up differently.

In fact, in some cases you could go from a 35 percent tax rate to as low as 5 percent (maybe even 0 percent) if you convert a taxable, ordinary-income asset to a long-term capital gain asset and gift that asset to your grandkids. They can cash it in at their 10 percent or 15 percent tax bracket (if they're over age 14—otherwise, the "kiddie tax" may kick in). That's a tax-rate reduction of 30 percent or more—a pretty *big* number!

But unless you're an investment expert, you're probably not going to know enough about the ins and outs of tax planning and tax-managing your investments to make these kinds of changes for yourself. That's why it's critical that you have an advisor or an advisory team to go through all this stuff with you.

A Powerful Incentive

The lure of paying less tax can be a powerful incentive when you set up your *Buckets*. Figure 8.1 shows how much more quickly a

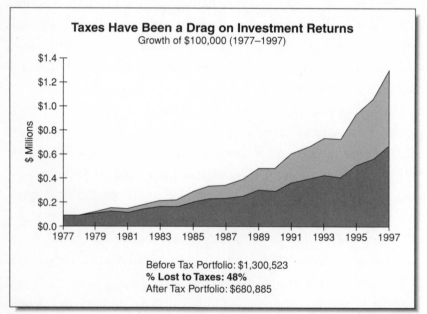

Figure 8.1

tax-deferred account grows over time. As a result, sometimes you may wish to split your *Buckets* between qualified (tax-deferred retirement accounts like an IRA) and nonqualified (taxable, personal money) retirement accounts, or have sub-*Buckets* divided into retirement money and non-retirement money. The most recent tax law changes underscore this need to be tax-savvy. With the tax on capital gains and dividends being reduced to 15 percent, it makes even more sense that your *Buckets* be structured so that your income-producing assets, such as bonds, CDs, and REITs, are in tax-deferred accounts and your stock is in personal, taxable accounts.

With our progressive tax system, it's sometimes wise to pull money out of a qualified retirement plan because you're already in a low tax bracket even if you aren't old enough to avoid the pre-age-59½ penalty tax (10 percent). Take a case like this: A guy, age 54, has been making a $100,000-a-year salary but wants to semi-retire. He figures he needs something close to $70,000 a year to live, starting now for the rest of his life. He's got $575,000 in his IRA invested for growth (earning about 10 percent) and $200,000 in personal assets in CDs at 5 percent. His Social Security won't kick in for at least eight years.

Further, let's say he's started a part-time job that will pay $3,000 a month, or $36,000 annually. He has $30,000 in mortgage interest each year as well as other tax deductions (such as property tax, dependents, and the like) totaling $20,000. Thus, he's got $50,000 in write-offs.

Needing $70,000 a year to live on, he's got to come up with $34,000 more on top of his part-time salary. Where should that money come from? Most would say take it from the personal money and let the IRA grow. But I question that. If he takes the $34,000 from his personal account, he is essentially in a negative tax bracket. His situation would look like this:

Salary	$36,000
Interest on CDs	10,000
	$46,000 total income
Minus write-offs	−50,000
Taxable income	(4,000)
	0 taxes owed

This is foolish and not very tax-efficient. Although he's not paying any income tax, he's also not very close to his income goal of $70,000, either. He can't carry forward to succeeding years those unused personal exemptions and deductions. But what he could do, however, is switch the $200,000 in taxable CDs into tax-managed growth accounts—and then leave them alone for the foreseeable future.

Then he can withdraw the needed $34,000 per year from his IRA account, which could be invested in a moderately safe portfolio. By doing so he creates enough ordinary income to use up the deductions in his low tax bracket. (Now you're probably wondering: How can he tap into his IRA without a penalty if he's not yet 59½? He does so by taking out substantially equal payments over his life expectancy under what's known as a 72(t) election. More about this in the next chapter.)

Under this new plan, his situation would look like this:

Salary	$36,000
Interest/dividends (from	
tax-managed portfolio)	3,000
IRA distribution	34,000
	$73,000 total income
Minus write-offs	−50,000
Taxable income	23,000
	$ 3,100 taxes owed (approximate)

Do you see how he's been helped? Sure, he now pays about $3,100 in taxes, but he's moved a lot closer to his income goal. And his mix of assets hasn't changed. He still has $575,000 invested in the stock market earning 10 percent and $200,000 in CDs at 5 percent. The only thing that's changed is the way the personal money and IRA money are allocated.

There are two further advantages:

- Some of the income from the $575,000 that now comes from the personal account will be taxed as capital gains, not ordinary income. Under current law, that means a maximum tax of 15 percent if you're in the 25 percent or higher tax bracket.
- If he should die and his assets were held properly in trust, there may be a complete step-up in the tax basis in his personal account. His spouse or heirs may never pay income tax on the gain from the $200,000 to whatever it grows to by the time he dies.

On the other hand, if he doesn't elect a 72(t) distribution and lives off his personal money, by the time he qualifies for Social Security, all of his nonsalary and investment income will come from his IRA account. That's because he already will have spent all his personal income. Furthermore, his deductions will be lower, part of his Social Security will be subject to taxation, and when he reaches 70½, his RMD (required minimum distribution) will be higher.

If he continues to live a long time and didn't do the 72(t), he will face substantially more in income taxes at full retirement, especially if his house is eventually paid for and he loses that income tax deduction. Or, one spouse could die, leaving the surviving spouse in a much higher tax bracket. Also upon full retirement, when he presumably quits the part-time job, he will need to withdraw the full, inflation-indexed $70,000 less his Social Security.

All of this will then need to come out of his IRA, possibly sending him into a higher tax bracket. Whereas if he takes the needed money now out of the IRA and invests the rest, he will be able to dramatically lower his taxes later. The point of the exercise is to match the type of investment owned with the type of tax that's going to be paid.

A Second-to-Die Sub-Bucket

Here's another twist to the Bucket No. 3 setup, one I call the *second-to-die* sub-bucket. It's an especially good way to pass along the largest amount of inheritance with the smallest amount of tax.

A lot of folks fail to take into account the effect of inflation on their estates. For instance, you might have $500,000 you're planning to leave your kids. And you diligently protect and preserve that sum for many years. The trouble is, those years of inflation take a toll. And when you die—say, 20 years later—that half mil isn't what it used to be. In purchasing power, you will have left your kin barely 50 percent of what you intended.

What you can do is take some earnings from Bucket No. 3, such as the dividends paid out from the stock portfolio or REITs, and use this money to purchase a second-to-die life insurance policy. It insures both lives but pays off only at the second death. Thus, when the remaining spouse dies, the insurance proceeds can be used to (1) pay the estate taxes, if any; (2) replenish the Bucket No. 3 assets you've depleted over time; and/or (3) give your progeny an inflation hedge on the assets they inherit.

If you want a policy that is likely to mirror the performance of equities in Bucket No. 3, you could purchase a second-to-die *variable* life policy. It usually has a guaranteed death benefit (as long as you meet a minimum premium requirement), but the cash value depends on the performance of the underlying subaccount, such as mutual funds. That way you're not giving up a whole lot from an investment return standpoint. The cash values can be invested in the same kind of model portfolio as your Bucket No. 3 would be invested in anyway.

A legacy sub-bucket works best for folks who probably won't spend every last dime of earnings from their long-term portfolio and who want to leverage their nest egg to keep pace with inflation and perhaps give their kids or grandkids a head start on their own financial security. It's an excellent way to go if you're in that situation, but it's complicated and you'll probably want to consult a team of advisors, including a tax attorney, CPA, CFP®, CLU, ChFC, or qualified life insurance agent.

Another Scenario

I am showing such examples not because they are a must for your *Buckets*, but rather because I want you to see why it's sometimes wise to use multiple *Buckets* within *Buckets*. That way, you can draw income from the most advantageous sub-bucket.

Here's another tax-planning scenario: If you were in a high-tax bracket (35 percent), you might put your Bucket No. 2 money in tax-free municipal bonds. In a market like the one we had in the spring of 2001, when interest rates seemed to be headed down, a short-term or intermediate-term municipal bond probably would be better for Bucket No. 2 than a tax-deferred annuity.

On the other hand, if you're drawing Social Security and trying to avoid paying taxes on those payments, tax-free municipals don't work so well. That's because the income they produce is an add-back to your modified adjusted gross income (MAGI), but the income from tax-deferred annuities is not. So if you were trying to get your Social Security tax-free, an annuity will work better than municipals.

Theoretically, you can even add bonds to your Bucket No. 3, although I usually don't recommend that. Why? Because we're investing for long-term growth. Unless you think bonds will add more to your return through added diversification, diluting your Bucket No. 3 with bonds isn't usually a good idea. Some conservative investors may want to look at some long-bond strategies in this *Bucket*. But in my opinion, they can be as volatile as stocks and may not give you the stability and growth you're seeking. Besides, to make real money in bonds you either must use leverage (borrowing) or timing, neither of which I recommend. If you must use bonds in Bucket No. 3, stick with foreign and junk bonds if you haven't already funded part of Bucket No. 2 with them. They will provide more diversification and potentially a better return over the long run.

What Does It All Mean?

It means you probably can't do this stuff yourself. You need professional help if you're to get the best bang for your buck. The strategies are as varied as the situations. But here's one inviolate rule. Let's call it . . .

LUCIA'S LAW 26

Thoughtful indecision is a key to flexibility.

In other words, stay nimble. Don't lock yourself into any one plan because your brother-in-law did, or because of something I wrote in this book, or because taking action—*any* action—seems better than contemplation. *Think,* and then go over all the options with your financial advisor.

CHAPTER 9

Managing Your *Buckets* in Good Times and Bad

Let's say you've got your *Buckets of Money* all set up. So life is good and going according to plan. And then something happens!

It might be something *good*—like a rare stock-buying opportunity, a chance to get a great piece of real estate, or inheriting some money. Or it might be something *bad*—such as prolonged poor health or a big tax liability. Or maybe it's neither good nor bad but just a contingency you must deal with—for example, you reach the age when you can, or must, draw down your IRA.

Any of those situations probably will prompt you to reexamine your *Buckets* plan. And in this chapter we'll look at what to do if those special circumstances arise.

If You Have Good News

A stock-buying opportunity presents itself. If the stock market plummeted 40 percent—not a theoretical possibility but a fact in

2000–2002!—and you've got a good chunk of safe money in your Bucket No. 2, what could or should you do? You obviously could do nothing, and that would be just fine. That's why we have safe money in Bucket No. 1 and Bucket No. 2, to get us through the rough spots. But usually the six months or a year or so after a market crash are very, very good recovery periods.

For individuals who can tolerate a bit more risk and possibly want to spice up their overall return, "reverse bucketing" may be a way to go. Thus, you could borrow some of your safe money in Bucket No. 2 and temporarily put it into Bucket No. 3, which is usually invested in a stock portfolio or mutual funds.

If the stock gods are in your favor and if the market bounces back in a year or two as it often—*but not always*—does, you may be able to significantly enhance your wealth or, if nothing else, get back some of your losses from the recent decline. Later you could pull that money out of the equities in Bucket No. 3 and replenish your Bucket No. 2. It's like buying low and selling high. As previously stated, most bear markets are followed by a significant gain over the ensuing 18 months to two years. The idea of reverse *Bucketizing*, although not for the faint-hearted, may be just what you need.

Of course, you would have to pay capital gains tax on those profits. But even so, depending on how much you invested and how well those stocks did, you might earn enough in a couple of years to give you perhaps four or five more years' worth of safe money in your Bucket No. 2.

This is a high-risk, potentially high-reward strategy that's not for everyone—and it certainly shouldn't be done often or without a great deal of thought. But potentially—if you and your advisor decide to try it and all goes well—you could reinvigorate your *Buckets* and give yourself added years of safe, reliable income. In essence, you'd be taking a half-step backward in your Bucket No. 2 scenario in order to take a great leap forward.

Again, let me be clear: I'm not in favor of trying to time the market. But in cases of severe market downturns, like the 1973–1974 decline or the tech wreck of 2000–2002, stocks became relatively cheap. An investment made anywhere near the bottom likely paid handsome returns. Besides, you wouldn't take 100 percent of Bucket No. 2 to do this unless you had a number of years of safe money in Bucket No. 1 producing the required income.

Another example might be getting a windfall. Let's say your aunt dies and, much to your surprise, leaves you $100,000. How could you use that to bolster your *Buckets*? Well, that would be a nice problem, and there could be several equally pleasant solutions.

You could plunk the whole $100,000 into your Bucket No. 3 and let it grow. If you could afford to do so, that would be the best long-term solution. That would work best if your Bucket No. 1 is churning out the income you need and your safe investments in Bucket No. 2 are doing what they're supposed to do, which is kick out a predictable, compounded return. If that's the case, then you can afford to squirrel away your inheritance on stocks and/or real estate in the long-term third *Bucket*. Depending where you are in the *Buckets* cycle and how it's working, you also could put some of your inheritance into Bucket No.1 and/or Bucket No. 2. For example, if inflation and expenses have drained Bucket No. 1 faster than you expected, perhaps you can give that *Bucket* a big boost with some of auntie's money. That also would buy added time to allow Bucket No. 2 and Bucket No. 3 to grow.

Maybe your Bucket No. 1 is producing the income you need, but you're worried about how much you're going to have in Bucket No. 2 when the time comes to empty it into the first *Bucket*. So maybe you'll want to use part of the inheritance to pump up Bucket No. 2.

Whatever you decide to do with your new-found gain, remember that *Buckets of Money* is a long-term philosophy. A central part of that means putting a big chunk of money in Bucket No. 3

and leaving it there for as long as you can. So, blessed with a windfall, think long-term, Bucket No. 3 as much as possible.

If You Have Bad News

Sad to say, not all our surprises are pleasant ones. You might also hit a big bump in the road. Let's take a look at how you might adjust your *Buckets* if that should happen. For instance, what if a prolonged illness raises its ugly head? Maybe it's not even you who gets sick, but perhaps your parents or another family member. In any event, your earlier financial planning should help solve these problems. If that planning was done correctly, you should have talked to your advisor about such contingencies. You should have made it a point to provide for long-term health care for yourself and your family, taken into account your parents' situation, and learned the Medicare rules and how Medicaid works in a long-term care situation.

Let's say you did all that, and *still* you're facing some big, unexpected costs, maybe hundreds of thousands of dollars worth. You must quickly figure out how to increase income and immediately change how your *Buckets* are structured. At that point you may have far more risk than you bargained for. Your Bucket No. 3 is loaded with stocks and maybe the market is rising nicely and your equities are doing well. But if your income needs to go up by, say, $3,000 a month to care for an ailing parent, you can't take the chance that the market won't flip-flop. You need to have a lot more safe money in case Wall Street quickly heads south. (We all know what happens when you have to pull money from a stock portfolio that's declining—you accelerate the loss. Just ask anybody who had to sell Intel stock in the year 2000 or 2001 just to live.)

So you're probably going to want to reapportion a good chunk of your Bucket No. 3 money into Bucket No. 1 and Bucket No. 2. How much? Enough to get you through this financial crisis. If that hypothetical $3,000 more a month will do it, then you can pretty easily figure how much more you're going to need in your Bucket No. 1. But don't forget: You're not just trying to meet your new obligation. You also want to lessen your exposure to risk by decreasing your Bucket No. 3; you can't continue to face that much risk when your need for current income is so acute.

Another path to consider is drawing down more of your IRA money. If you're over 59½, you could always opt to take a larger monthly distribution. (For most individuals, medical expenses that exceed 7.5 percent of their adjusted gross income are deductible. So taking taxable funds out of your IRA could be offset in part by deductible medical costs, making the bulk of the IRA distribution tax-free.) The IRA distribution rules are there to make sure you withdraw the bare minimum; you can take out *more* than that. Even if you're not 59½, tapping your IRA and paying the 10 percent penalty (there usually isn't a penalty if the IRA distribution is for medical costs) or using a 72(t) election might be worth it if the consequences of not doing so are sufficiently severe.

Other alternatives might include taking out a home-equity loan, borrowing against your brokerage account, or in a severe case, even signing up for a reverse mortgage in which, in effect, you'd be drawing down the equity in your home to get you over this financial rough spot. (Reverse mortgages usually are not available if you're under age 65.)

Any way you slice it, this crisis is a sorry state of affairs. Bucket No. 3 should be growing, not shrinking. But sometimes you gotta do what you gotta do. With any kind of luck, perhaps the cash emergency will be short-lived, and soon you can restore your *Buckets* to their proper proportion.

Another negative possibility is a big, one-time liability. Maybe it's not a medical emergency that slams you, but a financial one. Perhaps you're on the losing end of a lawsuit or are hit with a huge tax judgment or some other kind of setback that requires you to come up with cash, lots of cash. Again, I would hope that financial planning would include the right kind of insurance for such a situation. But if it didn't and you need to raise the cash by dipping into your *Buckets*, how would you do it?

Sad to say, you've probably got to dip again into that well we call Bucket No. 3. You need the assets in Bucket No. 1 to keep you in daily necessities. And that's backstopped by Bucket No. 2. So it's got to be No. 3 unless you are able to borrow some or all of the needed money, or the stock market has just gotten creamed and it makes more sense to risk giving up some of your safe money in Bucket No. 2 during the temporary setback. If, on the other hand, the market was on the rise and you expected it to continue its climb, you might consider borrowing at least part of the needed money if you had reason to believe your Bucket No. 3 stocks would grow at a faster clip than the interest rate on the loan.

However, as we know, this is a bit tricky. The stock market side of that equation can change in a heartbeat. And you could be left with a much smaller Bucket No. 3 as well as big loan payments. Be careful!

Drawing Down Your IRA

A more common dilemma is what to do with the *Buckets* when the time comes to start withdrawing your IRA money. As the law now reads, you *may* start that process when you reach 59½ years old. But you *must* do so when you become 70½.

Of course, being an IRS rule, it's much more complex than that. If you withdraw before age 59½, you'll likely get slapped with a 10 percent federal penalty in addition to federal and state taxes and maybe even a state penalty as well.

For all IRAs except the Roth, you must begin to withdraw the money by April 1 of the year following the year in which you turn 70½. (Failure to make the timely withdrawal will cost you—*are you ready for this?*—a 50 percent penalty, although there's currently some talk of reducing this.) The withdrawals—or *distributions* as they're known—are intended to last a lifetime. So you base your distributions on your (or your spouse's) life expectancy. IRS Publication 575—"Pension and Annuity Income"—includes tables you can use to dope out your required distribution.

To use the simplest of examples, if the tables show you have 20 years to live and your IRA is $200,000, you would be required to take out (and be taxed as ordinary income by both the feds and the state) at least $10,000 this year (1/20 = 5 percent × $200,000 = $10,000). The following year your minimum distributions increase (1/19, 1/18, 1/17, etc.) and if your account grows, you'll have to take out even more money.

The Fallacy of Common Wisdom

How you withdraw your IRA money and how you structure your *Buckets* for taxes will dramatically affect your retirement income. The common belief is: "Defer, defer, defer your taxes for as long as you can. Live off of your savings and don't tap into your IRAs until you absolutely have to at age 70½."

This mantra is accurate for some and foolish for others. Or, as I sometimes say . . .

LUCIA'S LAW 27

Absolute rules are created to allow us to escape thinking in exceptional situations.

Or, its corollary . . .

LUCIA'S LAW 28

Fools rush in where fools have been before.

In short, deferring the withdrawal of IRA money accounts always makes sense—*except* if you can take money out in a low tax bracket now instead of a higher bracket later. For example, let's say we have a married couple, age 62, with $50,000 in a money market fund for emergencies as well as $200,000 in CDs. They have another $200,000 in stocks in an IRA. In addition, they receive $18,000 yearly in Social Security benefits and have a pension that pays them $18,000.

According to conventional wisdom, they should live off of the income from their $250,000 in bank accounts (the $50,000 in emergency money plus the $200,000 in CDs) and continue to invest their IRA in stocks until they are forced to take minimum IRA distributions at age 70½. Their income and tax situation now looks something like this:

Now

	Receive Yearly	Amount Taxable
Pension	$18,000	$18,000
Social Security income	18,000	9,000
$50,000 money market (at 5%)	2,500	2,500
$200,000 CDs (at 6%)	12,000	12,000
$200,000 IRA (stocks)	0	0
Total income	$50,500	$41,500
Minus write-offs/personal exemptions		−16,500
Taxable income		$25,000
Tax due		$ 3,050

On the surface this looks great. The IRA isn't paying out yet—it's compounding tax-free as IRAs are supposed to do. Meanwhile, the couple is in the 15 percent tax bracket and paying only $3,050 in taxes each year. Even if they *Bucketize* the $250,000 in personal assets, their tax situation will not change dramatically.

Assuming their stocks earn 12 percent over the next 8½ years (when the couple both turn 70½), their IRAs will be worth something on the order of $500,000. Based on the IRS tables, they will need to make a minimum distribution of about $20,000 in the first year and increasing every year thereafter. Thus, if they remain on the present course, their situation would look something like this in eight years:

At Age 70½ If Stay on Present Course

	Receive Yearly	Amount Taxable
Pension	$18,000	$18,000
Social Security income	18,000	15,300
$50,000 money market (at 5%)	2,500	2,500
$200,000 CDs (at 6%)	12,000	12,000
$500,000 IRA (stocks) RMD*	19,100	19,100
Total income	$69,600	$66,900
Minus write-offs/personal exemptions		−18,300
Taxable income		$48,600
Tax due		$ 6,590

*Required Minimum Distribution

Thus, adding that $19,100 IRA distribution will cause their tax bill to more than double. They'll pay federal taxes of $6,590 versus the tax of $3,050 that they were previously paying.

Let's take a look at how they might do better with a smart *Buckets of Money* strategy. What they could do is:

- Put the $50,000 emergency fund in a tax-free money market fund. That'll reduce the interest, of course, but also will contribute to reducing the tax bill.
- Convert the $200,000 in CDs to a well-diversified, tax-managed, all-stock portfolio with the objective of long-term growth subject to long-term capital gains tax when sold. They would call that their Bucket No. 3.

- Convert the IRA stock assets into safe investments funding Bucket No. 1 and Bucket No. 2 (for example, bonds and CDs) and take the income from the IRA to meet their needs, at least to the extent of using up their 15 percent tax bracket. (It's good to use up that money now because otherwise the income will be received in the 25 percent bracket later.)

Under a scenario in which we tax-manage the portfolio but keep the income roughly the same, the couple's situation for the next eight years would look something like this:

Now—If Tax-Managed and *Bucketized*

	Receive Yearly	Amount Taxable
Pension	$18,000	$18,000
Social Security income	18,000	9,000
$50,000 tax-free money market (at 3%)	1,500	0
$200,000 tax-managed stock portfolio (Bucket No. 3) (figuring 1.5% dividend partially reinvested)	3,000	3,000*
$200,000 IRA with CDs and bonds (at 6%) (Buckets No. 1 and No. 2)	12,000	12,000
Total income	$52,500	$42,000
Minus write-offs/personal exemptions		−16,500
Taxable income		$25,500
Tax due		$ 2,825

*Taxed at 5 percent

Although the couple still has roughly the same amount to spend ($52,500 versus $50,500), they have positioned themselves better for that time when they must draw down their IRA. They also effectively used the 15 percent tax bracket to their advantage in structuring their *Buckets*. With this new, tax-managed structure, their situation at age 70½ (when they must start taking distributions from their IRA) will look like this:

At Age 70½—If Tax-Managed and *Bucketized*

	Receive Yearly	Amount Taxable
Pension	$18,000	$18,000
Social Security income	18,000	9,000
$50,000 tax-free money market (at 3%)	1,500	0
$470,000 tax-managed stock portfolio (Bucket No. 3) (figuring 1.5% annual dividend partially reinvested)	7,050	7,050
$200,000 IRA with CDs and bonds (at 6%) (Bucket No. 1 and No. 2) RMD*	7,635	7,635
Total income	$52,185	$41,685
Minus write-offs/personal exemptions		−18,300
Taxable income		$23,385
Tax due		$ 2,808

*Required Minimum Distribution

Note that the IRA distribution can be reduced as the dividend on the stock portfolio increases. This is good because the couple meets their income needs without additional distributions—and thus, without additional taxes.

The bottom line? They'll pay less than half the tax ($2,808 versus $6,590) per year when they turn 70½ than if they hadn't restructured their income.

Another Big Advantage to IRA Withdrawal

There's another big advantage this hypothetical couple would get if they took income out of the IRA while investing personal assets for growth. That happens when the husband or wife dies.

If they had stuck with the original, non-tax-managed plan, the surviving spouse would have had to pay more than double the amount of income taxes. Assuming one spouse dies at 70½, that picture would have looked like this:

At Age 70½, Surviving Spouse, Non-Tax-Managed Accounts

	Receive Yearly	Amount Taxable
Pension	$18,000	$18,000
Social Security income	12,000	10,200
$50,000 money market (at 5%)	2,500	2,500
$200,000 CDs/bonds (at 6%)	12,000	12,000
$500,000 IRA (stocks) RMD*	19,100	19,100
Total income	$63,600	$61,800
Minus write-offs/personal exemptions		−14,700
Taxable income		$47,100
Tax due		$ 8,585

*Required Minimum Distribution

Compare that to the tax bite the surviving spouse faces if the couple had gone to a tax-managed *Buckets* plan:

At Age 70½, Surviving Spouse, Tax-Managed Accounts

	Receive Yearly	Amount Taxable
Pension	$18,000	$18,000
Social Security income	12,000	10,200
$50,000 tax-free money market (at 3%)	1,500	0
$470,000 tax-managed stock portfolio (Bucket No. 3) (figuring 1.5% annual dividend partially reinvested)	7,050	7,050
$200,000 IRA CDs/bonds (at 6%) (Bucket No. 1 and No. 2) RDM*	7,635	7,635
Total income	$46,185	$42,885
Minus write-offs/personal exemptions		−14,700
Taxable income		$28,185
Tax due		$ 3,878

*Required Minimum Distribution

In addition, the surviving spouse has access to the $470,000 in the stock portfolio free of capital gains taxes. That's because assets held properly in a personal account may receive a full step-up in tax basis upon the death of a spouse; assets held in an IRA do not. Thus, if the pair had stuck with the non-tax-managed plan, the stock portfolio then in the IRA would have been taxed upon receipt by the survivor or the ultimate heirs. That tax could be as high as 35 percent federal, plus a potential state tax as well.

The point is, it's crucial to study the impact of taxes on each *Bucket*. A further point, of course, is that it makes sense to have a professional advise you before setting up any *Buckets* plan. That's because, as in this case, there are taxes on Social Security, taxes upon death, and ordinary income versus capital gains issues that really must be addressed. The right advisor and a good plan can increase your rate of return by simply shuffling your assets to the proper *Buckets* and applying tax management.

Getting Beyond the Box

As the popular phrase goes, sometimes it pays to think "out of the box." For example, even if you're under 59½, there may be times when it may be advantageous to draw down your IRA.

Let's say you're 53 years old and have an IRA balance of $200,000 as well as another $200,000 in personal money. You need $1,000 a month, and you're in a low tax bracket because of business-loss carry forward.

You might be able to employ IRS Code Section 72(t), under which you can annuitize the withdrawal of money from your IRA without having to pay a penalty. If you're 53, you have roughly a 30-year life expectancy. Figuring a 4.5 percent growth rate on your IRA (growth rates are specified and issued by the IRS monthly), you could expect to withdraw about $12,000 per year or roughly $1,000 a month.

If you could take $1,000 a month out of your IRA penalty-free and that came out in the 15 percent tax bracket, you could let the $200,000 in personal money grow at long-term capital gains rates and have it be tax-free at death. That might turn out to be a plus.

Another example: You're a 50-year-old with $600,000 in an IRA and $350,000 in personal money. You want to retire or semi-retire, and you need $30,000 to $40,000 a year to live on. Your life expectancy is 33 years. Figuring a 4.5 percent growth rate (issued by the IRS monthly), you could take $35,000 annually out of the IRA before you're 59½. That's taxable as ordinary income, but there are no penalties for these early withdrawals if you use the 72(t) election.

In this example, you invest your $350,000 in personal money for growth. By the time you're 59½, your personal money, which let's say has been growing at 9 percent, is now up to $795,000 (and will be taxed at the lesser capital gains rate when withdrawn, or will be tax-free at death). Your IRA is still around $600,000 (or more if the actual earnings rate is higher than the 4.5 percent rate used to determine the payout).

What have you accomplished? Well, in addition to having enjoyed the $35,000 per year to live on, you still have $600,000 in IRA money and $795,000 in the more tax-efficient personal portfolio once you reach age 59½.

If you hadn't done the 72(t), you would have depleted your personal account by age 64. Meanwhile, your IRA would have grown to about $2.6 million by the time you reach 70—which means you'd be forced to take a minimum distribution in a higher income tax bracket. If you died at 70½, your heirs would get the $2.6 million subject to a tax of around $750,000, less than what they would have received from the personal account invested in stocks with a step-up in basis at death.

In another example, say you're 49 years old and have all your money—$400,000, let's say—in IRAs. You have no personal investments. You want to diversify, so you're thinking of buying a condo or an apartment building. You've got a 34-year life expectancy. Figuring 4.5 percent interest factor for the calculation on your $400,000 IRA, you could, under Code Section 72(t), draw down your IRA by $23,000.

You could take this $23,000 and rediversify into real estate. Why is this a good idea? Because if you buy real estate with your personal (not IRA) account, you would get long-term capital gains tax treatment. Further, you would have leverage on the real estate as well as depreciation and other tax deductions. Thus, with a relatively small investment, you could control property worth much more and get added tax benefits. That, of course, accelerates the potential for return.

Consider yet another example. If you wanted to buy a serious piece of real estate, you could even borrow, say, $300,000 at a bank (perhaps secured by home equity) at a cost of about $20,000 a year, then put that $300,000 as a down payment on a $1 million property. To help you make the mortgage payments, use the IRA 72(t) drawdown to pay off the loan over time. If you've got real estate that produces 5 percent cash flow and appreciates 3 percent annually, you would be earning $80,000 a year on a $20,000 investment. And in this example, the $23,000 withdrawn from the IRA under 72(t) would be offset by investment interest deduction on the $300,000 loan, reducing the tax liability on your 72(t) distribution. Obviously, this is a risky strategy that's not for everybody. But it could produce a heckuva rate of return if you can find the right property.

Making Dreams Come True

I had a situation not long ago where a couple with three small children wanted to move to a larger home but were afraid the new mortgage would be too steep to handle. They had very little cash

personally but had handsome IRA and 401(k) plans. We decided
that living today was just as important as living well at retirement.
So we spun off enough money into a separate IRA, did a 72(t) election, and produced a $1,500-per-month, penalty-free distribution.

They were used to paying $3,000 a month in mortgage costs.
The new home mortgage cost was $4,500 per month. So it worked
out perfectly because their 72(t) IRA gave them just what they
needed. This distribution was taxable, but the extra interest they
were going to pay on the new mortgage offset the taxable income
from the IRA.

They're now living happily in their new, larger home. The
kids play in the new yard, and the whole family swims in the new
pool and enjoys barbecue on the new deck—all without financial
stress because their out-of-pocket expense is identical to what it
was in the old house. I was clearly their hero, which is why I *love*
doing financial planning. Every so often you can watch dreams
come true!

As for their retirement: If their $450,000 home appreciates
at the same rate as comparable houses, they would have simply
swapped some IRA money for some tax-free capital gain when
they sell their home and retire. They get to live today without sacrificing tomorrow.

The Classic Case

The whole idea is to take money out of your portfolio with the
least impact on taxes. That's why we use the *Buckets* or even frac-
tionalize the *Buckets* based on how much income we'll actually need
to live on and how much we think our overall assets are worth.

The classic case is a teacher or government worker. He or
she typically has a defined-benefit pension, a 401(k), a 403(b),
or some similar kind of pretax retirement savings plan, possibly
a pretax deferred compensation package (457 plan) and personal

IRAs. So, basically, every penny he or she takes out of those assets upon retirement is taxable.

This individual really needs to begin saving some post-tax money. Perhaps he or she could take advantage of Roth IRAs for tax-free growth if left alone until after age 59½. Even reducing the amount of discretionary dollars invested in pre-tax plans makes sense if you take an equal amount and invest it in a post-tax account. This way, one builds both pre- and post-tax assets so when it comes time to *Bucketize*, you can blend these two assets in order to reduce the tax bite.

The moral of these stories isn't that you should be intent on drawing down your IRA before age 59½ or that you should jump into real estate or jump into anything else. The point is that the possibilities are infinite, depending on your aspirations and the acumen of both you and your advisor. One of the major tasks you'll want to use your advisor for is finding a strategy that will work for you whether you're fully retired and need your investment income to live on, or are in the preretirement phase and want to enhance your income today or upon retirement.

Finding the Right Withdrawal Strategy

Too few people know—or think much about—how to plan their investment withdrawals during retirement. *Buckets of Money* is a sound, conservative strategy that helps you avoid the common mistake of having either too little exposure to stocks (thus, lacking protection against inflation) or too much (making you overly vulnerable to market whims). But it's not a guaranteed money machine; it still needs to be managed prudently. So when the time comes to draw down your IRA and/or Bucket No. 3, beware of averages. Averages—such as the stock market's long-term average annual gain of 10 percent—are helpful, but they can be hugely deceiving. (Remember the old joke about the guy who had his head in the oven and his feet in the refrigerator? *On average,* he felt quite comfortable!) The future is never exactly like the past. In truth, there are few average years, and variables abound—including how long you will live, the market's rise and fall, and the pace of inflation.

So how much can you safely withdraw from your portfolio each year? Probably less than you think. Why? Because the average stock market results are just that, an average. It's a mistake to just focus on the long-run average rates of return and not think about what can go wrong.

Further, even if a year did turn out to be average, that doesn't mean *your* return will be. Not everybody will enjoy the same good returns. Some investors will get significantly below-average results. That's *why* it's an average!

When you look at returns over, say, 50 years, the ups and downs sort of balance out. But when you start pulling out money in retirement, those ups and downs really matter. Let's say you have a $500,000 stock portfolio. You know the stock market grows long term an average of more than 10 percent a year. So you figure you can withdraw $50,000 a year and still keep a half million in your account. But that first year the market dips 20 percent (a relatively modest decline by recent standards), and your total falls to $360,000 (deducting your $50,000 plus 20 percent of the remaining $450,000).

If the market and your account bounce back 20 percent the following year, the *average* market gain/loss for the past two years is 0 percent. But your account is at only $382,000 after you take out another $50,000. Despite what the averages say is a break-even couple of years, you're down $118,000 that you may never get back. In fact, if the market has several such bad years while you're still taking out 10 percent, you could go broke in a surprisingly short time!

Further, the sequence of the returns also matters. Whether the up years come at the beginning, middle, or end of your retirement years makes a big difference. For example, retire just before a bull market, set up your *Buckets*, and you may live well and pass on a handsome sum to your heirs. Retire just before a bear market and with the same nest egg, same three *Buckets*, and same spending rate, and you could easily outlive your money. Again, that's because you're going to be drawing down on a shrinking amount.

In short, real life is more chaotic than your pocket calculator indicates. So you need to work carefully with your financial planner on various scenarios that anticipate a few shocks along the way. Here are some suggestions to take into that meeting:

- Assume you'll live to 100.
- Run several projections, including some with very conservative returns, so you get an idea of the range of outcomes you might face. Do the calculations year by year with actual returns rather than the average return for the period. (Ask your adviser to use something called *Monte Carlo simulation*. This takes into account a number of random performance scenarios and gives you the probability of success or failure.)
- Expect a long-term return of no more than 8 percent to 9 percent on your stock investments after you retire. (If that turns out to be low, you can attribute the jump in value to your brilliance as an investor!)
- Get your planner to show you how, by adjusting the mixture of stocks and bonds in your portfolio, you can affect the probability that your money will last as long as you do. Then choose a risk factor that's comfortable for you.
- If possible, plan to withdraw no more than 4 percent to 5 percent per year of your diversified portfolio's growing value.

This won't produce a fixed income, but it should help prevent
you from running out of money.
- Tax-manage your portfolio.

Work with your planner and respect his or her judgment. But
make it clear you'd rather be safe than sorry.

Obviously, a key in all this is to hire a really sharp, talented
advisor, someone who understands the architecture of your financial plan and the architecture of investments. That kind of knowledge and flexibility counts for a lot. In fact, in some cases it can
even make up for investment underperformance.

How do you find such a person? We're going to look at that in
Chapter 12.

CHAPTER 10

Repairing the 'Hole' in Your *Bucket*

For those of us saving for retirement, the stock market's 2000–2003 plunge—the deepest bear market since the Depression—was painful. If you're already retired or nearing that point, it was probably downright disastrous to your wealth building. As a former president used to say, "Ah feel your pain!"

In fact, almost every day I hear poignant stories from folks who find their fears soaring as their retirement assets plummet. That's not surprising—the bear market wiped out trillions of would-be retirees' wealth, and one survey in 2003 showed a full third of Americans weren't sure of having enough money to retire comfortably.

You may be one of them. It may seem to you as if your *Buckets* are leaking big-time, especially your Bucket No. 3. That was supposed to be a long-term growth vehicle, but now it's looking pretty sad, and you may not have the luxury of decades before you need the money. So, far from thinking of retiring early, you now worry about whether you'll be able to afford retirement at *any* age.

Maybe you got off to a late start saving for retirement. Perhaps your *Buckets* exist more as a concept than a reality. So you're thinking, *Bucketize what?* My retirement assets evaporated!"

What should you do? Well, for starters, try not to fret. Don't focus on what might have been, or pin your hopes on some miracle cure. Instead, take solace in the fact that if you already have or are preparing a *Buckets* plan, you've got a leg up on most people. You need, first, to take heart. And, second, take action to repair the holes in your *Bucket*. Here's how:

1. Find out exactly where you stand.
2. Save as much as you can in the years leading up to retirement.
3. Shed your debts.
4. Make lifestyle changes.
5. Consider delaying or modifying your retirement plans.

1. Find Out Exactly Where You Stand

Have you really been paying attention? Have you actually crunched the numbers? Or have you let your account statements languish unopened in a drawer somewhere and never quite gotten around to writing down your overall plan?

If so, now's the time to get serious about examining your financial health. Be prepared to revisit your financial goals. Double-check your assumptions about inflation, interest rates, and your longevity, and evaluate your progress toward your goals. Among the questions to ask:

- *How healthy am I?* What's my expected longevity? In one recent survey, only 11 percent of Americans correctly identified the average life expectancy of someone 65 years old today to be over 85; most underestimated it by five years or more. We all hope to live to an old age, but a longer life brings with it the risk of outliving your savings and other income sources. To guard against that risk, you'll need to estimate your life expectancy. You can use government statistics, life insurance tables, or a life expectancy calculator to get a reasonable estimate of your life span. (Many such calculators are available online. One that asks a few questions and then estimates your life span is at *www.livingto100.com.*) Longevity estimates are based on your age, gender, race, health, lifestyle, occupation, and family history. But *remember,* these are just estimates. There's no way to predict how long you'll actually live, but with life expectancies on the rise, it's probably best to assume you'll live longer than you expect.

- *Have I rebalanced my assets recently?* Do you know what proportion of your portfolio you need in stocks, bonds, and cash equivalents such as savings accounts and money market funds? Do you have a plan for achieving that mix? A key is to settle on an investment mix that you will stick with. You don't ever want to be in a situation where you lose your nerve and abandon your target portfolio percentages at the worst possible moment. The temptation, if you've had big losses (and *who* hasn't?), is to swing for the fences. Go for the hot sectors, the high yields. But if you're anyway near retirement age, that's a no-no. If you strike out, you may not get another turn at bat before it's time to retire.

- *Am I eligible for a traditional pension?* How much of one? Does it include a cost-of-living adjustment? Does it end when you die, or will your spouse continue to receive it? If you are eligible, your employer's human resources department can give you an estimate of the monthly benefits. In addition, get an estimate of your Social Security benefits by visiting the Social Security Administration website (*www.ssa.gov*) and ordering a copy of your statement.

■ *What other assets will I be able to draw upon?* Additional sources of retirement income may include a 401(k) or 403(b) plan, IRAs, annuities, and other investments. And, of course, if you plan to work during retirement, your job earnings will be another source of income. Also, is an inheritance likely or possible? If so, how big? Do you have assets you can sell to help fund your retirement? A vacation home, perhaps, or an antique car, an art collection, or other property?

■ *Do I want to leave assets to my loved ones?* How much? In what form?

■ *Do I know what my expected retirement expenses and income will be?* Soon-to-be retirees, especially, need to be as specific as possible. More on that below.

Please do your best to nail down the answers to these questions. You'll be better off knowing where you stand than just guessing or eyeballing it. Here's hoping that you may be pleasantly surprised by what resources you discover. In fact, research suggests that those who have calculated their retirement savings are nearly twice as confident about their prospects as those who haven't.

Mapping Out a Budget

If you're nearing retirement, you need to begin mapping out a budget—how much will you be spending each month? My advice: Don't put much store in those clichéd formulas that say you need 80 percent (or 70 percent or 90 percent) of your preretirement income to live on once you stop working.

Some mutual fund firms, stock brokerages, and financial advisors throw out those kinds of percentages because—*surprise!*—such lofty numbers may scare you into doing business with them. Only by buying their products or advice, they argue, can you hope to avert the crisis of not reaching the Magic Number. Of course, there is no Magic Number—or at least not one that makes sense for all of us. Sixty percent might be fine for me because I'm a frugal guy with hefty savings and I'm going to inherit my parents' house in a no-income-tax state. You, on the other hand, with one kid yet to send to college, a mountain of debt from educating the others, and a mortgage payment that would choke a horse, might find 75 percent impossible to live on. In short, one-size-fits-all doesn't work when it comes to retirement planning, or for that matter, almost anything else involving money. We need thought, not formulas.

A nationwide survey in 2001 by several economic researchers came to two conclusions: Many people are wrong about how much it will cost to retire, and proper planning can protect against those mistakes. So it's important that you be as precise as possible in calculating how much you'll need. Whether you do the math yourself or work with an advisor, include inflation and put the plan in *writing*. (Verbalized financial plans are, as Yogi Berra might have said, not worth the paper they're written on.)

Use one of the many when-can-I-retire calculators on the Web. (Most of the big mutual fund firms, such as Schwab, Fidelity, and Vanguard, offer them. Another well-regarded one is at *financialengines.com*.) These help assess your expenses and income and project how long your retirement savings will last.

Expenses

A big part of the retirement planning puzzle is, of course, estimating your expenses. For most people it costs less to be retired than still working. Why? Well, for one thing, you don't have to save for retirement because it's already here.

Beyond that, keep in mind that these expenses may change from year to year after retirement. For example, you may pay off your home mortgage or your children's education early in retirement while health care and insurance costs may increase as you age. To protect against these variables, build a comfortable cushion into your estimates. To help you get started, here are some common retirement expense categories and some points to ponder:

- *Food and clothing:* Because you're no longer going to work, you probably won't be spending as much on clothes. But will not having a company expense account mean you'll pay for more lunches?
- *Housing:* Rent or mortgage payments, property taxes, homeowners insurance, and property upkeep and repairs. Even if you pay off your mortgage, you'll still have taxes, and they likely will go up.
- *Utilities:* Gas, electric, water, telephone, and cable TV.
- *Transportation:* Car payments, auto insurance, gas, maintenance and repairs, and public transportation. Will you drive less because you no longer commute to work? Or more, because you'll be taking more driving vacations? Can you get rid of one car?
- *Insurance:* Medical, dental, life, disability, and long-term care.
- *Health care costs not covered by insurance:* Deductibles, co-payments, and prescription drugs. Figure on these increasing significantly as you age.
- *Taxes:* Federal and state income tax, and capital gains tax. Will you drop into a lower income tax bracket even after you

start receiving a pension, distributions from retirement plans, and Social Security? Remember, if you have no earned income, Social Security and Medicare payroll taxes no longer are levied; that's money that will accrue to your bottom line.

- *Debts:* Personal loans, business loans, and credit card payments.
- *Education:* Children's or grandchildren's college expenses.
- *Gifts:* Charitable and personal.
- *Savings and investments:* Contributions to IRAs, annuities, and other investment accounts. Is it likely you'll be making withdrawals, not additions? If so, that will boost your disposable income.
- *Recreation:* Travel, dining out, hobbies, and leisure activities. These probably will increase greatly with your added free time. Including the costs of volunteering, if you expect to do much of that.
- *Care for yourself or others:* Costs for a nursing home, home health aide, or other types of assisted living. This is where your long-term care insurance can really pay off.
- *Miscellaneous:* Personal grooming, pets, and club memberships.

Income

Add up the amount of income you can be sure of receiving, such as Social Security benefits, pension checks, and annuity payments. Next, you (and/or your financial advisor) can figure out how much money you can afford to withdraw from savings in employer-sponsored 401(k) or 403(b) plans, IRAs, or any other place where you've stashed funds for future use.

Withdrawing money from tax-deferred retirement plans is governed by your need and the Required Minimum Distribution

(RMD) rules. So retirees need to become familiar with those, or find a financial advisor who can guide them through this sometimes complex process.

2. Save As Much As You Can in the Years Leading Up to Retirement

A disciplined savings program offers a chance to regain control of your finances. *What?* You think you don't overspend? Guess again. In most budgets, there's plenty of room to cut costs. The U.S. Department of Labor estimates that in the year 2000, the average household spent over $38,000. Where did it go? Well, for starters, $319 was for tobacco, $372 for alcohol, $1,863 for entertainment, more than $5,000 for food, and almost $7,000 for cars. Gambling also eats up a bunch of dollars. Another study concluded that the average household gambled away $600. So there's probably some wiggle room in your spending patterns.

Meanwhile, the government encourages you to prepare for your future—and lower your tax bill—by contributing to your employer-sponsored retirement account. But even if your employer doesn't offer a retirement savings program, you have good options. They require you to do some planning, which a lot of people find difficult. In fact, one survey, by the Employee Benefit Research Institute, found that only 37 percent of workers have even attempted to calculate how much they need to save for retirement, down from 51 percent in early 2000.

Recent tax law changes allow you to save far more than before in tax-advantaged 401(k) plans and IRAs. That's especially true for workers who have reached their fiftieth birthday. For them, 401(k) and 403(b) contributions can be as much as $20,000 per year by 2006 (and Congress is considering accelerating that). For IRA holders over 50, the limits are being raised to $6,000 by 2008. So you can set aside large sums in tax-advantaged plans. In fact, finding enough money to save may be the real challenge.

My suggestion: Don't scrimp until it hurts. Don't go without an occasional night out or something you really enjoy. Instead, integrate saving into your lifestyle. Make it an organic part of what you do. Don't cut out all the luxuries, or you may feel so deprived that you scrap your savings program.

How much should you be saving? One rule of thumb suggests 10 percent of your pretax income every year. But in truth, the right number depends on your situation. If you will receive a traditional company pension, you may not need to save that much. On the other hand, if you started late to build up your retirement accounts or lost a ton in the last bear market, you may need 15 percent or even 20 percent or more because you've got fewer years to save and fewer years to garner investment returns.

Here are some savings ideas I'd recommend:

- *Bolster your contribution to your employer's 401(k) or 403(b) plans.* It's a great way to compel yourself to save because the money is pulled out of your paycheck before you get a chance to spend it. Even if you don't have an employer plan, many banks have automatic investment plans in which the money is deducted from your bank account every month and invested directly into mutual funds you choose. If your employer matches your contribution up to a certain level, it's doubly foolish not to contribute up to that limit.
- *See if you or your spouse is eligible for an IRA.* After you've put away the maximum in your 401(k) plan, check to see if you or your spouse can contribute to either a traditional IRA or a Roth IRA. If you can and if neither you nor your spouse is covered by an employer-sponsored plan, you can usually

deduct from your taxes the full amount of your contribution to a traditional IRA. If one of you is covered by a plan and the other is not, there's a good chance the uncovered spouse could fund a deductible IRA if your income is less than $150,000. The deduction phases out from $150,000 to $160,000. Otherwise, any couple earning less than $150,000 can contribute to a Roth. (Roth contributions also phase out from $150,000 to $160,000.) Contributions to a Roth IRA aren't tax-deductible, but the proceeds are free from taxes.

- *Invest any windfalls.* Any nonrecurring sums—bonuses, inheritances, tax refunds, medical insurance reimbursements, money from a second job, or you name it—should be stashed for retirement. As far as living expenses go, just pretend that you didn't get these pennies from heaven. Because this money isn't part of your regular income, it's a fairly painless way to save.
- *Forego third paychecks.* If you're paid biweekly, then there are two months each year when you receive three paychecks. Put some or all of that away for retirement.
- *Capitalize on tax cuts.* The top four federal income tax brackets were lowered by 2 percent in 2003 and more cuts are scheduled. You could painlessly increase your savings rate by an equal amount in each of those years. Also, the 15 percent bracket has been expanded for married couples, putting more money in your pocket to save.
- *Save your raises.* If you get, say, a 2 percent raise, bank it. Or increase the deferral rate to your 401(k).
- *Cut insurance costs.* Whether it's home, life, auto, or health, you may be able to cut your premiums without sacrificing service or coverage. The Internet makes it easy to get competitive quotes, and you can also lower your premium by raising your deductibles.

■ *Slash the little things.* Look for a bank that offers free check-ing. Avoid ATM service charges. Find a cheaper Internet ser-vice provider. Drop the premium cable channels. Shop around for lower telephone rates. Decide if you can do without your cell phone. What about brown-bagging your lunch or giving up that daily latte or renting a movie instead of going to the theater?

The GE Center for Financial Learning recently worked up some figures for how much you'd save by forgoing some of those small luxuries and investing that money for 30 years at 8 percent interest. For example:

Item	$ Saved	Savings Over 30 Years (at 8 percent)
Bring coffee to work instead of buying it	$1/day	$ 32,241
Brown-bag lunch	$5/day	$161,455
Rent video in lieu of theater	$15/month	$ 22,355
Give self manicure instead of salon	$20/month	$ 29,807

Even just saving your change each day, the study said, would net $2/day or $64,482 over the long term. Sure, I know you probably don't have 30 years to save. But the point is, small steps can lead to big savings. Think about it.

3. Shed Your Debts

Many families spend a big chunk of their income to keep their creditors at bay. The result is less money available for retirement savings. So get your home-equity loans, auto loans, and credit cards paid off, and you'll have more financial room to maneuver. Making this change is easier if you start planning for the transition well ahead of time.

The Consumer Federation of America says that the average balance for households that carry credit-card debt from month to month is more than $10,000. Credit-card debt is the least desirable because the interest rates are very high, and the interest you pay isn't tax-deductible. My advice: Put the plastic away. Think about the true cost of your purchases, including the debt service.

Consider refinancing at a lower interest rate to free up money to save for retirement. But don't take money out of your home equity unless you're going to use it to pay off higher-cost debt. And *don't* draw down your home equity to get money to invest—unless the investment has substantial upside and almost no downside. If you find one like that, call me!

Of course, getting rid of debt means making tough choices—and that means you won't get everything you want. Maybe you won't be able to travel overseas or help buy your kid a home or have a new car every few years. That's what sacrifice entails.

If you adjust to a tighter budget now, it could have a two-edged benefit. First, you'll be able to save more for retirement, and second, once you're used to living on less, you'll need less income in retirement.

Whatever you decide, you'll want your partner on board. If one resents the deprivation, that's a recipe for trouble.

4. Make Lifestyle Changes

You may not want, or need, to significantly change your lifestyle. But if you're willing (or *desperate!*), some of these suggestions, if enthusiastically embraced, could help jump-start your retirement plans:

- *Opt for a simpler life.* Could you retire earlier or more comfortably if you lived on more of a bare-bones budget? Many do. But that, of course, means spending a lot less. Are you the kind of person who could substitute a canoe trip for a Caribbean cruise? A used car or even a bicycle for a fancy new auto? The constraint of cash for the ease of a credit card? If your partner is willing, you could embrace a simpler lifestyle. This could be as small as planting a garden, or eating at home rather than dining out.

- *Downsize your home.* If you're willing to sell and move to a less expensive home, you can plow the profit into your retirement account. Thanks to tax law changes, you won't owe taxes on the first $500,000 in capital gains if you're married and have lived in the home for two years or more. (For single taxpayers, it's $250,000.) In addition, you'll probably have lower property taxes on the new place and perhaps less maintenance.

- *Move to a less expensive part of the country.* That means giving up friends and familiarity. But if it's something you've wanted to do anyway, you might be able to make some money on the property and stash it away. (If a move beckons, go to *www.bestplaces.net* and click on "find your best places to live.") Be sure to take into account how high the taxes are in your new state or even find a state-tax-free locale.

- *Make sure you're looking out for No. 1.* Sure, it'd be nice to leave your kids a bundle. But if times get really rough, don't let that ideal drive you to the poorhouse. Lighten up on their legacy if that's the only way you can enjoy a reasonable retirement. Explain your options; I feel sure they'll understand.

- *Put on hold plans to save for the grandkids' college.* If your kids are already in school, notify colleges of a change in your financial circumstances. That could qualify you for a revised financial aid package.

- *Take out a reverse mortgage.* Maybe you're sitting on this huge chunk of cash but you don't want to sell the house and move because you like it and the neighborhood. After all, that's why you've stayed there so long. A reverse mortgage would yield you a lump sum of cash or a predetermined monthly amount. The amount you receive depends on your age, the amount of home equity, the interest rate charged by the lender, and the closing costs. To repay the loan, you or your estate will need to sell the house or turn it over to the mortgage lender. It's called a *reverse* mortgage because, unlike a traditional mortgage, the principal balance gets larger over time, not smaller. It works best for those who wish to stay in their homes until they die. How much could you get? One such calculator is offered by AARP, the seniors' group, at *www.rmaarp.com.* But before you jump at the idea, investigate the downsides. Those include reducing your home equity (probably one of your biggest assets), high closing costs, and tax impacts. Although a reverse mortgage is not for everybody, it may be a boon for some. For example, for retirees facing a serious lack of income, reducing their equity may be better than reducing their standard of living to the point where, say, they don't have enough to eat.

- *Get a de facto reverse mortgage from your kids.* If your children are doing okay financially, you might be better off working out a deal with them. If they're going to inherit your home, would they be receptive to helping you out with a reverse mortgage? They might be able to kick in $500 or $1,000 a month from their own home-equity line of credit. They become the reverse mortgage lender without the fees. They can deduct the interest they pay and make a gift to you for what you need (not to exceed $11,000, or gift taxes apply). After your death, they get the house as an inheritance free of any capital gains tax. It's worth talking to them about.

5. Consider Delaying or Modifying Your Retirement Plans

Let's say you've taken a good look at the state of your nest egg. Further, you've ramped up your savings, pared debts, and made as many lifestyle changes as you can handle. But the numbers still don't add up to a comfortable retirement. *Now what?*

It may be time to concede, NASA-like, that "Houston, we have a problem" and prescribe a midcourse correction for your particular retirement odyssey. Maybe you shouldn't tie retirement to a certain age but instead only plan to retire when you have enough income. Who knows? Maybe that isn't at some traditional retirement age.

Naturally, the longer your retirement, the more income you'll need to fund it. So it'll cost you a lot more to retire at age 50 than at 65. Retiring at 50 or 55 may be ideal, but if a booming stock market and a generous early retirement package don't conspire to make that possible, then you've got to adapt. Maybe the chaise lounge next to a pool isn't where you can afford to spend the next few years. Some options may include:

- *Delay your retirement.* Continuing to work for a year or two or more can cause various things to happen, most of them good. Your savings will have more time to grow. Maybe you can pay off that pesky car loan and reduce your mortgage. Working also will allow you to postpone tapping your portfolio, giving your investments added time to recoup. And they wouldn't need to stretch as far because your retirement will be shorter when you start withdrawing from them. Plus, you'll also get a larger Social Security benefit. (Your check will be permanently increased for every month you delay taking benefits past age 62 until you reach 70.)
- *Retire but work part-time.* Maybe you were overly optimistic. Instead of having all that time to catalogue your stamp collec-

tion, maybe you'll need to work two or three days a week as a greeter in a Wal-Mart or spend summers slinging hash at a cafeteria in Glacier National Park. There are worse things, especially if you can work at something in which you have a passionate interest, whether it be teaching math or working with animals or just meeting lots of people by clerking in a shoe store.

■ *Scale back your regular job.* If you haven't yet retired and can't quite see how you're going to make ends meet, maybe you could transition by scaling back your hours and responsibilities. Employers are increasingly open to such arrangements. Ideally, this would give you a measure of control over your schedule and also provide the extra income you need to afford retirement. Keep in mind, though, that if your earnings exceed certain thresholds, they could reduce your Social Security benefits received prior to your full retirement age (65 to 67, depending upon your year of birth).

Scaling back also may allow you to maintain employee benefits, such as a 401(k), pension plan, and maybe health care coverage. (Health care insurance is an expensive benefit to replace if you retire before age 65, the earliest date at which most people become eligible for Medicare.)

Regaining the Luster

Time *will* heal the wounds of the early 2000s. Stocks, I believe, will once again regain their luster as the best-performing, long-term asset class. Remember, there have been numerous bear markets in the past 50 years, and somehow stocks still have been able to post average double-digit gains. The market has survived world wars, the Great Depression, hyperinflation, stagflation, a weak dollar, a strong dollar, and Republicans and Democrats.

Despite all of this, the U.S. economy continues to be the model for the rest of the world.

So if your *Buckets* are leaking, you do need to act, not just worry. Do what you need to do to get back in the game. But as you do so, keep in mind the role of the *Buckets*: to help you stay focused and to buy you the time needed to allow your stocks and real estate to grow. The *Buckets* strategy will continue to help you to clearly and specifically define your asset allocation and preclude you from selling stocks or bonds for income at inopportune times. That's an important edge.

CHAPTER 11

Bucketizing My Life

Okay, so you've repaired the hole in your *Buckets*. Great! Though hardly out of the woods, you're feeling a bit more secure. Now it's time to get down to the nitty-gritty of planning how the *Buckets of Money* strategy is going to produce a comfortable retirement income beginning when you need it *and* for as long as you need it.

If you're like most folks, you've probably got a jumble of assets, many of them acquired without too much thought about how they'll fit together in a decade or two. Some investments probably sit in taxable personal accounts while others rest in tax-deferred retirement plans. Maybe some pay dividends, and others offer only the hope of appreciation. Some kick out tax-free income, but on others, the IRS takes a healthy cut. Some of your assets, present or potential, depend on others—the government for Social Security, for example, or your employer for a pension. These require little action by you. But others are the result of your conscious choices, perhaps using assumptions about returns and interest rates that may no longer be valid and will require monitoring.

This chapter seeks to show you how to bring together those kinds of threads into a coherent plan, to demonstrate how the *Buckets* strategy can work for an actual person in a real-world scenario. To do this, I've used my own situation. Although I have modified my assets in the following example to a hypothetical $1 million and left out some of my investment property, the rest is true. And, it's hoped, instructive.

Who Is This Investor?

For starters, you need to inventory just who you are and where you are in your life's journey. In my case, I'm 53 years old, chubby but healthy nonetheless, and married 30-plus years to my sweetheart, Jeanne, with four grown children, ranging in age from 26 to 29. (The rhythm system didn't work for us, but that's okay; the kids are *great*!)

Other facts needed for analysis:

- *Retirement age*: 62, nine years from now. (That's also very hypothetical. I'll probably never retire because I'm having too much fun.)
- *Expected Social Security*: $15,000 at age 62. Jeanne's will add $7,500 later.
- *Investable assets*: $1,000,000 ($500,000 in IRA and $500,000 in a personal account).
- *Emergency fund*: $50,000 in cash.
- *Investment philosophy*: Conservative.
- *Legacy goal*: Leave as much as possible to our kids and to charity.

- *Needed retirement income*: $75,000 in today's dollars.
- *Expected inflation rate*: 2.5 percent.
- *Other income sources*: Two existing variable universal life insurance policies are expected to produce $25,000 in annual, tax-free income ("Legacy Bucket"), beginning in nine years. The annual premiums are $25,000.

Step No. 1—Manage Our Risk

Managing risk should be the first move in any financial plan. What risks? Dying prematurely, becoming sick or disabled, or losing a job, to name just a few. Let's look at how we would protect against those.

Dying Prematurely

Because I have more than $1 million in investable assets, my wife probably would be okay, but she wouldn't be as well off as I would like, at least not yet. Remember, I still have nine years before I retire.

I carry variable universal life insurance (VUL) policies and term coverage that total more than $1 million, but I will probably drop the term coverage after I retire. So I feel pretty good about Jeanne's security if I die too soon, and my two VULs should provide the added permanent insurance I want and also produce a tax-free income stream of $25,000 when I retire.

Becoming Sick or Disabled

I have disability insurance to supplement my income if illness or injury prevents me from working. However, long-term care (LTC) is something I'm concerned about. What happens if Jeanne or I end up needing home health care, convalescent care, or a nursing home? That could rapidly deplete our nest egg. So I recently met with an insurance agent friend who showed me how to take my low-yielding emergency fund of $50,000 and put it into a long-term care/life insurance policy. But I'm also evaluating a few periodic premium payment LTC policies, too. Maybe I'll end up doing both.

As my friend explained, that $50,000 in the emergency fund probably will never be spent unless the emergency is an illness or injury. (Because I'm self-employed with a decent income, I'm not worried about losing my job.) So he proposed putting that $50,000 into a principal-guaranteed second-to-die life insurance policy in which the death benefit of $300,000 could be used for either of us for LTC.

If we die before using that policy, the return will be similar to an ultra-short-term municipal bond. If I need access to the cash in a genuine emergency, I can borrow the cash value tax-free from the policy. (The insurer pays me about 5 percent on my $50,000 while it sits in the policy, about 3 percent of which goes to cover the cost of LTC and death benefits. So if we die, the kids get more than we put in tax-free.)

If we need the money for LTC, we can spend way more than we put in. And if we need the cash, we always have access to our $50,000, and over time a 1 percent or 2 percent return (potentially tax-free) isn't bad. So I'll probably buy that policy with my emergency fund money, which is only earning 1 percent to 2 percent taxable anyway.

Thus, by having both disability and LTC insurance, I'll effectively manage the risk of dying too soon or becoming sick along the way.

Step 2—Determine Our Risk Profile

I'm a relatively conservative investor. Why? Well, for one thing, I've watched many well-read investment pros lose a ton in the recent bear market. Some will need to postpone retirement 10 or 15 years in order to retire on the income they could have had if they had *Bucketized* in the year 2000. At age 33 that doesn't present a major problem; at 53 it does.

Here's what I know: Never has there been a 15-year period in which an investment in the broad market didn't at least produce a positive rate of return. And never in a 20-year period have stocks not produced a better return than the rate of inflation. So if I want a dollar in the market to be worth more than a dollar in purchasing power, I'll need to let my stock market money alone for 20 years.

Using a conservative *Buckets of Money* strategy for Buckets No. 1 and No. 2—and a 20 percent allocation to a low-leveraged REIT in Bucket No. 3—should buy me that 20 years-plus if I haven't rebalanced prior to that. Then I'll begin to liquidate some of the stocks in Bucket No. 3. Being conservative, I don't want to risk my retirement security by seeking to eke out a little better rate of return.

Step No. 3—*Bucketize*

As I said, I'll need $75,000 for retirement income, starting in nine years, less our Social Security and less the $25,000 annually I expect from the VUL policy.

I don't need present income, so I don't need a Bucket No. 1. But what I will need starting the tenth year is about $94,000. That's $75,000 in today's dollars times 2.5 percent annual inflation. So my income needs will look like this:

Years 1–9:   No income needed

Year 10*: $54,000 ($94,000 minus $15,000 Social
             Security benefit and $25,000 VUL)

Year 11: $54,000

Year 12: $54,000

Year 13: $46,500 (Jeanne's Social Security of
             $7,500 kicks in)

Year 14–20: $46,500

Note: For simplicity's sake, I didn't inflate my income needs each year,
beginning in year 10.

So the question becomes: How much money will it take to produce this needed income in nine years? Here's how I figure it:

Years 10–12

It'll take about $153,000 to fund $54,000 at 4 percent interest. But remember, I don't need that money for nine more years. So the present value of $153,000 nine years from now means I can invest $107,000 today to grow to $153,000 in nine years at 4 percent.

Years 13–20

Here I need $46,500 per year. Using the same type of calculation, I will need $318,000 to provide $46,500 for eight years, assuming I can earn 4 percent on my money. However, I don't need this money until the beginning of that thirteenth year. Again, using a 4 percent earning rate, I'll need about $198,500 today to grow for 12 years at 4 percent in order to produce the $46,500 that I'll need in years 13 through 20.

Adding those sums and rounding them up, I'll need about $305,500 ($107,000 + $198,500) today to provide the income I'll need in nine years and lasting until year 20 of my retirement.

So here are what my *Buckets* look like (Figure 11.1):

Filling Bucket No. 3

That leaves Bucket No. 3 to fund. This *Bucket* consists of a 20 percent allocation to REITs (that is, 20 percent of the entire portfolio, not just 20 percent of this *Bucket*), a VUL that I have owned for years, and the remainder in the stock market.

VUL

I'll continue to fund it annually at $25,000 per year. For now, the VUL is invested in an index fund that I'll later reallocate.

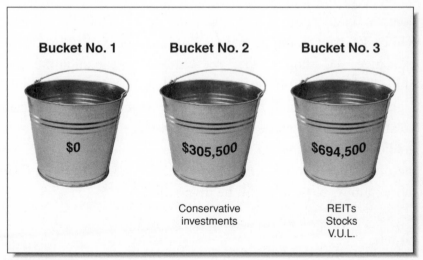

Figure 11.1

REITs

Ibbotson Associates, the Chicago research firm, studied REIT performance from 1972–2002 and concluded that a 20 percent allocation to equity REITs reduces risk and increases the potential for return long term. I happen to like low-leveraged REITs, ones without a lot of debt. In my case, I own a commercial office building REIT in which the buildings are owned mostly free and clear of mortgages. The tenants are Fortune 500–type firms on long-term, triple net leases. I get a 7 percent dividend but choose to reinvest it.

I also own a hospitality REIT, which consists of hotels leased out to major hotel operators (such as Marriott and Hilton) and an assisted-living REIT. (As the Baby Boomer population ages, the need for assisted living is likely to explode.) The dividend yield on these two is about 7.5 percent. But there is 30 percent to 40 percent leverage on these, so I expect a little better yield and a somewhat better overall return than on my office building REIT. But, clearly, there is more risk because there is more leverage.

None of my REITs are traded on an exchange, so the price doesn't fluctuate on a daily basis as do most publicly traded REITs. I expect that in the next few years mine will all list on the exchange, and I hope to then get a little extra capital at the time of the initial public offering. I'll probably sell at that time because I get enough ups and downs from my equities; I don't need volatility from my real estate, too. However, if you already own public REITs or a mutual fund of REITs, fear not—you'll still get the diversification that REITs provide. The road may be a little more bumpy, but you'll still be diversified.

Stocks

I've studied the markets for 30 years and have looked at all sorts of techniques: market timing models, technical analysis, star ratings, hedge funds, you name it. What I've learned is that active management beats indexing some of the time, indexing beats active management some of the time, and market timing, tea leaf reading, investing by astrology, and other fads just don't work—period.

So my only recourse is to apply what I know. First, I need an oversight manager—someone capable of designing the right asset mix of large- and small-growth, large- and small-value, mid-cap, international, and emerging markets stocks. Then I need to select the appropriate money managers and hold them on a short leash to make sure they don't drift from one style to the next. If they underperform their respective benchmarks, I need someone to understand why and decide to either hang in there with them—or hang them!

I asked myself: Who has an extensive database of money managers? Who is likely to do the best job as oversight manager for my Bucket No. 3 money? I went to one of the big mutual fund firms, and we came up with what we thought would be the best way to manage Bucket No. 3.

My idea was two-pronged: Put one half of the money in a concentrated mutual fund portfolio managed by high-Alpha managers (money managers who consistently add value above their benchmark), and put the other half in exchange-traded or index funds to broaden out the portfolio and potentially reduce the risk.

I liked the idea of professional management, using high-Alpha money managers. But I also wanted to make sure that at least part of my portfolio would reflect the actual performance of the benchmark. That way, if the Alpha goes negative and underperforms the benchmark, at least 50 percent of my stock-market money is indexed in low-cost, tax-efficient funds.

Of course, true *Bucketeers* leave Bucket No. 3 money alone for the long term. So the combination of high-Alpha funds and indexing should work well over the long run.

Here's my Bucket No. 3: $200,000 in three nontraded REITs, $494,500 in a concentrated Alpha/indexed portfolio, and a VUL that I'm funding at $25,000 a year (Figure 11.2).

Tax-Managing the *Buckets*

At this point I know I'll need $305,500 in conservative invest-ments for Bucket No. 2, but I haven't decided yet how to invest that money. The reason I'm unsure is that I don't know how much I'll want to draw down from my personal account at re-tirement and how much I'll want to take from my IRAs. This is where tax questions become critical. For relatively safe money in a personal account, tax-free municipal bonds and tax-deferred annuities may work best. Inside my IRA, mortgage bonds, corporates, certain fixed annuities, and junk bonds may be better choices.

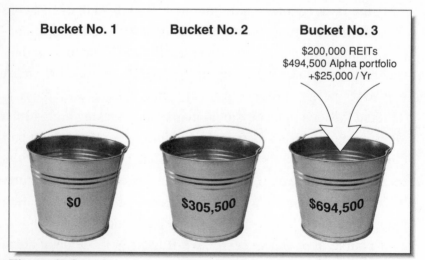

Figure 11.2

Let's review: I know I'm going to be living on $94,000 in nine years, but only $54,000 will need to come directly from the portfolio. That's because Social Security will provide $15,000 and my VUL will, it's hoped, provide $25,000 of tax-free income. By today's standards, Jeanne and I should be able to earn about $16,000 in the zero-percent tax bracket (because of standard deductions and personal exemptions). But let's assume a 2.5 percent inflation factor that would result in no taxes being paid on the first $20,000 of income—perfect for a withdrawal from the IRA.

The next $14,000-plus will be taxed in the 10 percent bracket. Maybe that's a good choice for retirement income, but we need to check the tax on Social Security as well. Under current law, when a married couple's modified adjusted gross income (MAGI) reaches $32,000, then up to one-half of their Social Security is taxed. Over $44,000, up to 85 percent of their Social Security is subject to taxation. So in my case, I want to be sure I manage not only my regular tax but also the tax on my Social Security. So let's check it:

	Income	MAGI
VUL	$25,000	0
Social Security	15,000	7,500
Maximum taxable distribution to stay under $32,000 MAGI	24,500	24,500
	64,500	32,000

So if I want to keep the taxes on my Social Security as low as reasonably possible, I shouldn't take more than about $20,000 from my IRA. That's because there will be some dividend and capital-gains income from the balance of the taxable portfolio in Bucket No. 3. So my VUL will provide $25,000, my IRA distribution $20,000, and Social Security $15,000. I'm short $34,000, and that will have to come from my personal account.

When Jeanne's Social Security kicks in three years after we retire, then we'll need only $26,500. So my Bucket No. 2 should be split between IRA and personal money, as shown in Figure 11.3

In summary, then, Bucket No. 2 will be divided with IRA qualified money of $125,000 and a personal, nonqualified portion of $206,500. At 4 percent, the $125,000 will spin off $20,000 per year of taxable distributions. Assuming 3 percent

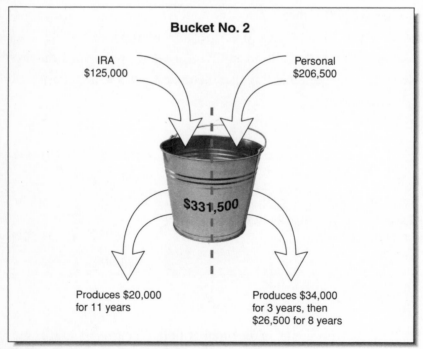

Figure 11.3

tax-free, laddered municipals, the nonqualified portion will produce $34,000 for three years and then $26,500 for the following eight years, all tax-free. (The municipal bonds give us a tax advantage. But because their 3 percent yield is less than the 4 percent we originally planned for Bucket No. 2, the total amount allocated to that *Bucket* has risen to $331,500 from $305,500.)

That leaves us with $293,500 of personal money (remember, we began with $500,000 personal and $500,000 in an IRA) and $375,000 of IRA money to invest in Bucket No. 3. The $200,000 in the REIT spins off a dividend of 7 percent or so, most of which would be taxable. So maybe it would be better to buy it with the IRA money. Everything else in Bucket No. 3 should be invested in equities—the balance of $175,000 in the IRA and $293,500 in the personal account (Figure 11.4).

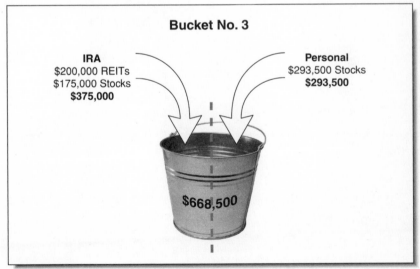

Bucket No. 3

IRA
$200,000 REITs
$175,000 Stocks
$375,000

Personal
$293,500 Stocks
$293,500

$668,500

Figure 11.4

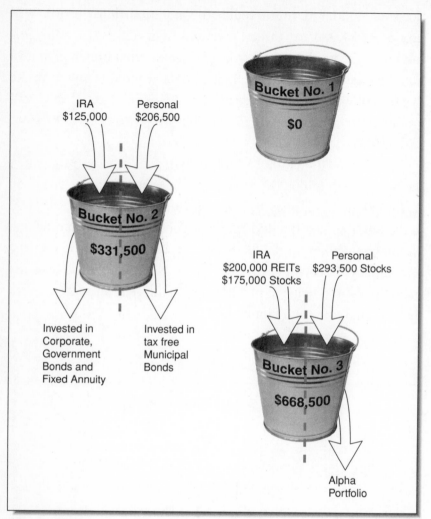

IRA $125,000   Personal $206,500

Bucket No. 1
$0

Bucket No. 2
$331,500

Invested in Corporate, Government Bonds and Fixed Annuity

Invested in tax free Municipal Bonds

IRA
$200,000 REITs
$175,000 Stocks

Personal
$293,500 Stocks

Bucket No. 3
$668,500

Alpha Portfolio

Figure 11.5

So here's what the overall *Buckets of Money* strategy looks like (Figure 11.5).

What's the Future Tax-Wise?

In nine years, how will we be looking tax-wise?

	Income	Amount taxable	MAGI
IRA distribution	$20,000	$20,000	$20,000
VUL	25,000	0	0
Social Security	15,000	7,500	7,500
Personal distribution	34,000	0	8,100
			(Interest)
Dividend reinvestment	0	6,500	6,500
	$94,000	$34,000	$42,100

Approximate federal income tax owed: $2,100.

So I'll be living on $94,000 a year in nine years, the inflated equivalent of $75,000 today (assuming 2.5 percent inflation). And I'll be paying very little tax on my *Buckets*. Not bad!

Meanwhile, what will my portfolio look like in 20 years? Let's take a peek: Assuming I don't tap into any more than $331,500 in Bucket No. 2 to spend from year 10 through year 20 (11 years), my Bucket No. 3 will be left to grow. Remember, Bucket No. 3 has $200,000 in REITs with an assumed 7.5 percent reinvested dividends and $468,500 in equities split between personal and IRAs (Figure 11.6).

While we might hope the stock market will deliver double-digit returns over the next 20 years, we'll assume 9 percent for these purposes. If so, Bucket No. 3 will reach $3,475,000. However, even if stocks produce a 7.5 percent return—roughly the same as a REIT—it'll still be worth $2,840,000.

A Dynamic Process

This has been a cursory look at how a *Buckets of Money* strategy potentially works. Clearly, a $1 million portfolio that grows to $3,475,000 in 20 years is pleasant to contemplate, but it's certainly not guaranteed. Nor is the Social Security payment or the

Bucket No. 3
20 years later

IRA
Stocks
$175,000
Growing at 9%

IRA
REITs
$200,000
Growing at 7.5%

Personal
Stocks
$293,500
Growing at 9%

$668,500

$850,000

$980,000

$1,645,000

Grand total = $3,475,000

Figure 11.6

other returns. That's why *Buckets of Money* is a dynamic process, not a plan you can just set and forget.

Lots of things could change that would skew these projections. For instance, at some point, I may—and probably would want to—take more money out of my IRA because eventually it could balloon to more than $2 million. At that point, my Required Minimum Distribution may force me to pay more tax than I want to. Similarly, the VUL returns may vary and thus I may not be able to withdraw $25,000 per year for life. What's more, some-one could die or need extensive care. Or I may want to make gifts to my kids or to charity that will decrease my nest egg.

While this isn't, as they say, rocket science, it isn't simple, either. Especially not when you add to the mix the possibility, perhaps even the likelihood, of the tax laws changing and upset-ting your calculations. Thus, as we'll see in the next chapter, a knowledgeable advisor can be a key ally in anyone's *Buckets of Money* strategy.

PART V

LIVING HAPPILY
EVER AFTER
AS A BUCKETEER

CHAPTER 12

Finding the Right Financial Planner

If you're uncommonly cool and clear-headed, you're probably thinking after reading the last few chapters: *Sure, I understand all that. Now let's get started with some serious wealth building!*

Okay, so much for fantasy. If you're like most everyone I know, your thoughts are more along these lines: *Arrgghhh! This is complicated stuff—all those situations, all those possible tax consequences, all those various strategies! How can I ever get a handle on this?*

How you can get a handle on it is by getting help. Most folks don't have the training, the time, or perhaps the temperament to do this kind of planning themselves. So if you want to do a good job with your portfolio, you're going to need to pick an able financial advisor or a team of advisors. Then you can sleep well knowing you've got a plan tailored for you and a portfolio that's fully diversified and minimally volatile.

Remember that broad diversification and a multi-asset, multi-style, multi-manager approach to investing is what will make your Bucket No. 3 work. And as a practical matter, you'll probably need an investment professional to help you attain that. In this chapter, we're going to look at ways to find such a person or persons.

For starters, let's review what we have said such an advisor would do. In general, he or she is someone who can help you take a step back and see the bigger picture, someone who can study your situation and devise a program that'll meet your goals. Specifically, the planner will:

- *Work with you to develop a plan.* This means, first, understanding your goals. Then, the advisor puts your plan and the recommendations in writing so there's absolutely nothing left for interpretation now or later. Next, the advisor selects the right kind of investments, insurance, estate planning, tax planning, trusts, budgeting, and other methods to reach those goals and fulfill the plan's recommendations.
- *Pick—or work with a money manager selection firm to pick good fund managers.* It's these money managers who will do the hands-on choosing of your specific Bucket No. 3 stock investments.
- *Hold those managers to their style discipline.* That might be growth, value, large-cap, or small-cap, but not overlapping.
- *Know how to judge a manager's performance.* Be familiar with the appropriate benchmarks and compare the managers' results to them.
- *Terminate those managers who consistently underperform relative to their benchmarks.* This isn't fun but is sometimes necessary.
- *Keep up to date with changes in the financial world.* That might mean changes in interest rates, changes in kinds of

investment vehicles, tax law changes, personnel changes in the money manager ranks or other changes.

- *Rebalance your investments.* The planner assists you in sticking to your asset-allocation model.
- *Tax-manage your portfolio.* The planner helps you keep your taxes as low as possible in relation to your other objectives.

Not surprisingly, you're going to need to spend some bucks to get this kind of help. But if you hire a really sharp advisor, his or her performance should pay for itself—and *a lot more.*

How do you find such a wizard? Well, first make sure you know what you're looking for. If you don't want a full-blown financial plan, and you just want someone to give you investment advice, then almost any planner or broker can do that. And in some states, almost anyone can advertise themselves as being a financial planner. So you won't have any trouble finding one if you're aiming for just, say, a stock or mutual fund picker.

But if—as I would strongly urge—you want a full-blown financial review and a real plan, you probably want to look for a CFP®, a ChFC, a CLU, a CPA, a PFS, or some similar designation. At the very least, look for someone working hand in hand with a skilled, credentialed advisor.

What Do All Those Letters Mean?

What the abbreviations stand for is not as important as what they signify in a broader sense—that this person took the time and made the effort to study the field, subscribe to its code of ethics, and take continuing education courses. But more important than the exact initials after his or her name is what kind of rapport you have with the planner, how knowledgeable he or she is, how interested he or she is in your situation, and how well you like and understand the plan he or she comes up with. Still, knowing a little about this alphabet soup may help you make a better choice.

First, some background. In the good old days, it was relatively easy to know where to go to for help. A banker loaned cash, an insurance agent sold insurance, and a stockbroker peddled stocks and bonds. But several things have happened to change that. One, a lot of new products got introduced—everything from annuities to junk bonds, from foreign currency options to pork belly futures. Secondly, new types of salespeople sprouted up to sell both the old and new investment vehicles. Further, the distinctions among those salespeople blurred, so that bankers now also sell stocks, stockbrokers now loan money, and insurance agents now can get you into all manner of investments.

Thus, the task becomes not only *what to buy* but *from whom to buy it.* That's one of the big reasons for the popularity of financial planners. At their best, they help you cut through the clutter and make the best financial choices. But just because a person is a financial planner—even a credentialed financial planner—doesn't guarantee a successful relationship.

The keys to finding the right financial planner include locating someone (1) whom you are comfortable with, (2) who is willing to explain your options, (3) who charges a reasonable fee or commission, and (4) who has enough experience to add value to your overall plan.

Of course, that's not as simple as it sounds because financial planners come in a lot of different flavors. For starters, there are those alphabetical designations. And then there's the question of how planners are paid. Let's take those issues one by one.

Alphabetical Designations

Some of the initials you see after a planner's name are there because of federal licensing requirements, whereas others represent ways the industry seeks to market its services. For example, planners who sell securities must hold a federal securities license. Most also are members of the National Association of Securities Dealers (NASD), a quasi-governmental agency that regulates the industry.

Any person who provides financial planning also must be a Registered Investment Advisor. That means he or she is registered with the Securities and Exchange Commission. The person did so by filing a form, paying a fee, and showing that he or she understands SEC rules. While you should never work with anyone who's not registered (because it's a federal crime to be an unregistered planner), neither should you take the designation oh-so-seriously because what it really means is that the registrant knows SEC procedures, not necessarily the finer points of financial planning.

The other designations are issued by the various financial industry associations, not by the government. Applicants must complete course work and continuing education, and meet other prerequisites to be awarded these designations, which include:

CFP®—This well-known set of initials stands for CERTIFIED FINANCIAL PLANNER™ and is earned by those who take a two-year course, pass a rigorous two-day examination, and meet continuing education requirements.

ChFC—Chartered Financial Consultant is a designation usually given to insurance agents or financial planners who undergo a two-year program and complete exams and continuing education. Many ChFCs are also CLUs, or Chartered Life Underwriters, which involves a similar course of study and continuing education.

CFS—A Certified Fund Specialist has taken a course and exam centering on the selection and monitoring of mutual funds.

CPA—A Certified Public Accountant is one who has passed a rigorous exam to certify his or her knowledge of accounting, auditing, and tax issues.

CMFC—Like CFS, this designation reflects the advisor's expertise in the mutual fund industry but stands for Chartered Mutual Fund Counselor.

CRPC—A Chartered Retirement Planning Counselor specializes in retirement planning issues.

RFC—Registered Financial Consultants must meet education and licensing requirements and take a minimum of 40 hours of professional education each year. That's roughly two to four times as much as the other designations require.

PFS—This designation as a Personal Financial Specialist is offered to Certified Public Accountants (CPAs) who pass a test or hold the CFP® or ChFC designation.

If your planner doesn't have any of those designations, then he or she at least ought to be working in tandem with somebody who does.

How Financial Planners Are Paid

A great deal is written in the financial press about how financial planners are paid: commission only, fee only, or some combination. I'm not so sure it matters all that much. But just so you'll be fully informed, let me explain the pros and cons of each.

First, understand the difference between a financial planner and, say, a captive stockbroker or insurance agent. Usually, but not always, the broker and agent will talk to you about their proprietary products and will give you lots of advice about which of their products might be best. Some proprietary products are just fine; others may be not so fine.

Independent planners, on the other hand, usually don't have proprietary products per se. What they do is take a comprehensive look at your situation, offer advice to help meet your goals, and then fill your needs with various nonproprietary products. But, as you'll see, most planners work for banks, brokerages, or insurance firms, or work as independent advisors. And they all pretty much sell the same types of products as insurance agents or stock brokers. Product sales aren't necessarily bad. After all, someone has to get you to act. But it's important for you to understand the compensation arrangement.

Commission-Only Planners

These planners almost always work for a bank, brokerage, or insurance company. But like planners elsewhere, they will ask about your income and expenses, your goals, your comfort level with risk, and so on before suggesting appropriate investments. They would argue that instead of paying two fees—one to hire a planner and one to a broker to buy the investments—you can do one-stop shopping. You can just hire the commission-only planner and only pay when he or she makes a transaction for you. Others contend the commission-only planner is naturally biased toward his firm's products and thus has a built-in conflict of interest.

I know and trust many commission-only planners who work for brokerages and insurance companies and do an excellent job. If you can find the right one, you may save some money in the long run. However, I also know a few whom I wouldn't trust with the equity in my old pair of wingtips.

Pure Fee-Only Planners

These planners get a fee to make the same kind of analysis and to give you recommendations. Much like an attorney, they charge for their service and their time. But because they have nothing to sell, you go to someone else to actually purchase the investment.

The planner's fee may be an hourly rate (say, $100 or more per hour) or a flat fee (perhaps several thousand dollars). They neither receive a commission nor place assets under management for a fee.

Advocates of pure fee-only planning say it's totally free of conflict of interest. But critics argue that you still need to pay a commission or sales charge to a broker to implement the plan. The fact that you're paying twice, they say, doesn't necessarily make the advice any better or the process cheaper or more pleasurable. In any event, these types of advisors or advisory firms are rare.

Fee-Only Planners

These planners make the same kind of analysis and give you recommendations, but they usually also charge an asset-based fee on the assets they place under management. Most belong to a professional organization and are held to very strict standards. However, "fee only" is sometimes disguised as a rolling, annual commission and may, in fact, turn out to be more expensive than if you paid a load in the first place.

Combination Fee and Commission Planners

This is a common arrangement (also called *fee-based*) in which planners charge you for the analysis, then sell you the investments and either receive a commission or a fee based on the assets under management or on how well your portfolio performs. These commission-like asset-management fees are preferred by some consumers because they avoid up-front commissions. Planners also like asset-management fees because they provide a steady stream of income, whether the investor is trading or not.

Where asset-management fees become a problem is when the percentage is too high (say, above 2 percent) and when yet other fees are tacked on.

Fee-Offset Planners

These are advisors who charge a fee, and if you choose to do business with them, rebate, or offset, the fee against their commission. This avoids double-dipping, but in some respect cheapens the plan itself and may skew it toward the products the advisor wants to sell.

Me? I don't think the whole debate amounts to much. In fact, I believe it's ludicrous to say that a fee-only advisor is necessarily better than someone who charges a commission. So many aspects of financial planning—such as integrity and knowledge—are so much more important. The truth is, you're going to pay either way, and in some cases you may end up paying more to a fee-only advisor.

So the bottom line is this: If you hire the right advisor, it shouldn't matter how he or she is paid. If the advisor does a good job, he or she will be worth the fee and/or commission. If he doesn't do a good job, then whatever way you paid the advisor will be misspent.

You don't want to overpay. For example, paying a 1 percent to 2 percent advisory fee for a portfolio that's 50 percent stocks and 50 percent bonds is outrageously high. If you pay a one-time commission to set up a bond portfolio, and then pay an asset-based fee on the stock portion, you've cut your fees in half. So be smart about what you are paying for. But as to the form of payment, who cares?

What I believe is more important is that planners disclose fully their financial arrangements. I'd almost like to see a new

"FD" designation, along the lines of CFP®-FD or ChFC-FD. The FD would stand for Full Disclosure, which means planners show prospective clients how they are paid, how often they are paid, and how much they are paid and by whom. That might be the most helpful designation of them all.

In any case, you should insist on full disclosure when working with any financial advisor.

Where to Find a Planner

Just as you would before hiring a plumber or a brain surgeon, make an effort to ask around. Query friends or co-workers whose judgment you respect and whose financial situation and risk sensitivity is somewhat akin to yours. Many advisors give free seminars. This can be a way to not only learn more about investing but also check out the planners themselves. These seminars often are advertised in the newspaper or on radio or TV or through flyers that come in the mail.

You could always use the Yellow Pages, of course, and the Internet now provides another way to connect with the right planner. Web sites for the big financial planning organizations, such as the National Association of Personal Financial Advisors (*www.napfa.org*) and the Financial Planning Association (*www. fpanet.org*), have search mechanisms to help connect you to their members who practice near where you live. In addition, MSN's MoneyCentral (*http://moneycentral.msn.com*) also has a device for helping you find planners by geographic preference. (As I write this book, I am personally credentialing *Buckets of Money* financial advisors to help out my radio listeners around the country. You can request information at *www.raylucia.com.*)

I have been teaching and training financial planners for more than 20 years. My litmus test for good advisors is this: If they can do retirement projections, tax management, and asset allocation right on the spot, there's a good chance they know their stuff. If they need their computer or home office to do the work, you should probably pass.

What to Expect

Good planners will draw out needed information from you by asking questions. Their aim will be to figure out your objectives. They may also request copies of wills, trusts, partnership or pre-nuptial agreements, insurance, employee benefit manuals, and investment information, and perhaps even ask you to draw up a budget and balance sheet listing everything you own and every-thing you owe.

But *you* ought to be asking questions, too. I recommend you interview at least three planners and ask them these 12 questions:

1. *How long have they been in the business and how long have they been in your community?* Planners who have roots in the community may be more cautious than johnny-come-lately's. Even more important is how long they've been planners. You want someone who's been around long enough to have suffered through a bear market. Prior to the bear market of 2000–2001, a lot of younger planners hadn't experienced such a downturn. As a result, you could run into, say, a talented, aggressive 27-year-old planner who forgot about safe money, forgot about value, threw caution to the wind, and really overexposed his clients to risk. Many folks right now are paying the price for that and may need to delay retirement because their planner, having never experienced that sinking feeling of losing a lot of his clients' money, was too aggressive. So you want to make

sure your advisor has enough experience to deal with your situation. You want him or her to understand how you need safety as well as growth.

2. *What will they do for you?* Design a plan? Implement it? Both?

3. *What is their investment philosophy?* This is important. You don't want to be force-fed financial choices. Be clear what your goals are and how you'll be most comfortable getting there. You want to be sure your planner understands modern portfolio theory—that is, asset allocation—and isn't just trying to time the market, use gimmicks, try out risky strategies, or bet your money on his or her ability to pick winner stocks.

4. *What kind of investments do they specialize in?* Be wary if they talk just about insurance, or limited partnerships, or mutual funds, or any one investment vehicle to the exclusion of most others. In short, you want someone who is planning-driven, not product-driven. Then, if the plan calls for one or more of the aforementioned products, you can respond accordingly.

5. *Who is their typical client?* Once you know that, then you can judge: Are you a good match with how much their average investor has to invest? Are you comfortable with roughly the same amount of risk? You also might ask to talk with some clients whose situations are similar to yours, especially those who have been through down years as well as up years with this planner. What you'll want to find out from those clients is not so much the state of their investments but the state of their relationship with the planner. Has he or she kept them informed? Done what was promised? Exceeded expectations in some ways? How? Disappointed in others? How?

6. *How will this relationship work?* Who will make the decisions—you or the planners? What kind of paperwork will

they send you? Do they require you to sign a contract? If so, how can you opt out if the relationship sours? How often will you meet face to face?

7. *How are they paid?* If by fee, what do the fees include? If by commission, how much will that likely be? Ask for a full, clear explanation because some planners claiming to be "fee only" actually receive commissions as well.

8. *Have complaints been filed against them?* Ask them directly. But also, especially if you have any doubts, check the National Association of Securities Dealers (if they have a securities license), the state insurance commission (if they have an insurance license), and the SEC (to see if they are Registered Investment Advisors). All planners are supposed to give you a copy of Form ADV Part II, which is a statement they file with the SEC about their background, methods, and fees. But you may have to ask for it. You can also ask to see Part I, which they are not required to show you. Part I discloses any history of criminality or regulatory sanctions as well as unsatisfied judgments, liens, and bankruptcies. Part I also tells the number of clients advised in the past year and total assets under management. The SEC is in the process of making Form ADV Parts I and II available more easily and quickly on the Web (*www.sec.gov*). Investment advisors will be required to file an electronic version of Form ADV. (A disciplinary history of brokers at firms who are members of the NASD already is available online at www.nasd.com. But unlike Form ADV, the NASD records don't provide information about fees, business practices, educational background, or potential conflicts of interest.)

9. *Will the planner draw up a letter explaining exactly what's going to happen, including planning services and fees?* This should be part of the full disclosure I mentioned earlier.

10. *Will they show you a sample financial plan?* Seeing this may help you decide if they are preparing thorough plans or just crunching numbers into a software program, a task you could probably do yourself for much less money.

11. *What assumptions are they going to use in your plan?* For example, will they use life expectancy as defined in some computer program—say, 78 years old—or will they use a more conservative approach and take you out to 100 years old or beyond? If they stipulate 78 and you live to age 100, those last 22 years could be rough! What kinds of market return assumptions are they making? If they project more than 10 percent annual return for stocks (net, after their fees), that's too aggressive. Similarly, what kind of withdrawal scenario do they foresee? I've seen cases where planners had clients taking, for instance, 8 percent a year out of 100 percent equity portfolios. That's nuts! One or two down years and that portfolio is going to shrink faster than an ice cream cone in Phoenix in July.

12. *Are they backed by a firm of size and stature?* Is the planner part of an organization of some heft and reputation? Or is it a rinky-dink outfit that, should there be trouble, won't be of much help? With any kind of luck, this is an issue you'll never need to put to the test. But it wouldn't hurt to find the answer to this question: If the planner did run away to Tahiti with your money, would you get reimbursed by his or her organization?

Other Things to Check Out

By using your eyes and ears when you visit a prospective planner, you can also connect some other dots. For example:

- *How big is the office and how is it run?* If the staff and office are big, that may be good but it'll also drive up costs. So be sure to ask about fees. If the office and staff are small, you could have trouble getting your calls returned. Does the office appear to be neat and organized? Neither too luxurious nor too spartan?
- *Do they explain things well?* Can they make it simple enough for you to understand? Or are they hiding beneath too many technical terms and a blizzard of statistics?
- *Do they talk about you first?* They should find out about you before moving on to products that they believe would be good for you. A product-first approach suggests a planner who's perhaps more interested in peddling something than in coming up with a plan that matches your goals.
- *Are they into fad investing?* If they're big on such things as, say, market timing or technical analysis, you should turn and run. And if they claim some proprietary method of picking stocks or use a lot of razzle-dazzle, they're probably not for you.

Getting Started with a Planner

Once you've found the financial planner for you, take good advantage of that opportunity. Be proactive, not passive. Seek to be a full partner in the discussions.

For starters, figure out how much income you're going to need from your Bucket No. 1. Don't necessarily take at face value those articles in the money magazines that say you'll need 75 percent, 60 percent, or 80 percent of your present-day income to live on when you retire. Instead, carefully review with the planner your current monthly cash flow. Factor in any costs you expect to incur down the road—more travel, perhaps, or different hobbies, or maybe a boat or a new car.

Then subtract any contributions you're now making to your retirement accounts and Social Security because you'll no longer be paying those once you retire. Also eliminate expenses normally associated with work—business clothes, lunches out, and commuting costs.

Subtract your mortgage payment, too, if your house will be paid for by then. But be sure to include inflation-adjusted home-owners' insurance and property taxes because those don't go away just because you pay off the mortgage.

Take into account you and your spouse's Social Security benefits and when you expect to receive them and, of course, any other benefits—like a company pension, an annuity, or an inheritance—that might kick in later.

Once you've figured out just what you're going to need in Bucket No. 1, it's just a matter of arithmetic to tally how much you'll need in Bucket No. 2. And the rest—by far the largest portion of your assets, I hope—goes into the third bucket.

Then comes the fun part—doping out what kinds of investments will meet your *Buckets* objectives. Be patient. Be persistent. It'll take a little time and effort to do this right, but it's time and energy well spent. In fact, much better spent than just fretting about the future but not doing anything about it. Or, as I sometimes say . . .

LUCIA'S LAW 29

It takes just as much energy to wish as it does to plan.

And its corollary . . .

LUCIA'S LAW 30

But planning is far more likely to produce results.

Planner versus Money Manager

How do they differ? In short, a financial planner is a big-picture person who helps you with your strategy and who, among other things, can put you in touch with a money manager. A money manager actively oversees your investments on a day-to-day basis.

Sometimes a planner is also a money manager. But if I were you, I'd steer clear of those. Either job is a demanding one, and the odds are not good that someone can simultaneously do both well. Further, money managers tend to become experts in their own investing style—say, small caps, growth, or value stocks— and by definition, you as a diversified investor will want your portfolio to span multiple styles, not be concentrated on one. The way to get that diversification is to have a financial planner who will help you draw up a plan, set up your asset-allocation model, rebalance your portfolio, help you manage risk, and make sure you have enough liquidity. Then that planner can hire style-specific managers to invest your money in accord with your plan. Those money managers choose and buy the actual stocks.

How does the planner find these money managers? He or she may hire them directly or may work through a money-manager selection firm, or both. Typically, it doesn't cost any more to go through a selection firm because their trading costs are kept low by the sheer volume of their business.

Once hired, the money managers must be monitored by the planner. The planner wants to make sure there isn't a lot of overlap with other managers and that the managers meet their benchmark indexes. If they consistently underperform, they aren't choosing very good stocks and need to be replaced. If they overperform, they may be too aggressive, perhaps using options strategies or buying, say, value when they're supposed to be buying small-cap stocks.

A Word about Wraps

A *wrap* in financial terms isn't a coat or a fancy sandwich or what movie directors say when they're done filming. Instead, it's an account that combines private management and trade execution. Available at most brokerage and planning firms, the wrap account usually requires a $100,000 minimum investment. Thus, in order to achieve diversification in seven or eight different asset classes, you'd need at least $700,000 or $800,000. That may make wrap accounts infeasible for many retirees. There are some asset-allocation wrap accounts for smaller sums, but most are quite expensive. If you can find the right wrap or asset-management account that is fully diversified and you meet the minimum investment level (usually $150,000), you may be set for your Bucket No. 3.

More important than what the account is called is what it costs. Wrap accounts too often include some extra costs. Whether yours is a wrap or asset-management account, you'll want to hold the total expense to under 2 percent annually of the amount invested—that's management fees, trading costs, everything.

One problem I have with most fully allocated wraps or asset-management accounts is the wrap fee is charged on the entire allocation. To me this defies logic. If I structure your *Buckets of Money* strategy using conservative investments like CDs, annuities, and bonds in Bucket No. 1 and Bucket No. 2, why would you pay an extra 1 percent to 2 percent for a broker to manage accounts that require no management.

By splitting your funds into three *Buckets* and paying a 1 percent wrap fee strictly on Bucket No. 3, you may be able to reduce your advisory fees by more than 50 percent. Simply tell your advisor to recommend bonds, CDs, and annuities for Bucket No. 1 and Bucket No. 2, and only pay him or her to manage Bucket No. 3.

A Final Word about Integrity

Most financial professionals are highly ethical and responsible. But, of course, they're not immune to the personal frailties that plague other professions. Knowledge is your best safeguard against deception and incompetence.

It'll be up to you to evaluate the planner's performance and assess his or her advice. You've got to remain alert. It's not enough to say, in effect, "Here's my money. Take good care of it for me." Remember, as long as the cost is reasonable and accountable, it's not how you compensate your advisor that's most important but rather how comfortable you are and whether you are meeting your goals within a stated risk tolerance.

Of course, you shouldn't ever sign a blank document or allow the planner to break the law by signing your name to anything. Don't give the planner authority to make transactions without your knowledge or consent. Don't agree to list him as joint owner or beneficiary on any of your accounts. And you shouldn't pay more than 50 percent in advance for planning work or pay for more than one quarter of asset management in advance.

Look out, especially, for any financial professional who promises a sure thing or the need to act quickly before it's too late. There are *no* sure things, and acting quickly without thinking causes many a financial debacle. And if you become dissatisfied, don't hesitate to change advisors.

CHAPTER 13

10 More Steps You Could Take to Help Bulletproof Your Retirement

Short of inheriting a zillion dollars, setting up your *Buckets of Money* plan is one of the smartest steps you can take to help ensure a comfortable retirement. But it's not the only thing.

Whether you're on the threshold of retirement or still decades from it, there's more you can do to pave the way. Achieving financial literacy is a lifelong process, and in this chapter, I want to outline other measures you can take or habits you can foster that'll serve you well in your later years.

Some of these ideas go against the grain, yet there's nothing magical or maybe even startlingly original about most of them. But because you've taken the time and made the effort to grapple with the *Buckets* philosophy, you may be hungry for other ways to help get your financial life in order. If *Buckets* is the main course, consider these to be financially healthy side dishes that only enhance the enjoyment of the entrée.

1. Start Early, Save Much, Live Long

Time creates money. Every so often, you read about somebody who died at age 104 and, despite working only as a dishwasher or a gardener, was able to bequeath maybe a million dollars to a favorite school or charity. Looking closer, you'll find that those folks started saving early, squirreling away their pennies and allowing the miracle of compounding to do its work.

Few investors ever have big sums handed to them via inheritances or gifts. Instead, they accumulate assets by working hard, by doing without, by managing well, and by accepting reasonable risks. All of us can learn from these poor but persistent savers.

The first lesson: *You can't start too soon.* In fact, to start saving at an early age is the best way to ensure a comfortable retirement. A 25-year-old who saves just $50 a week will have almost $763,000 by age 65, assuming an 8 percent tax-deferred return. If that same young person were to delay saving by just 10 years, he or she would accumulate by age 65 only $325,000—57 percent less. So the longer you invest, the more you'll reap the rewards. Yet, sad to say, among adults in their late fifties, median savings are less than $10,000.

Second, *be a disciplined saver.* Don't spend your gross salary because, as I like to say, if your outgo exceeds your income, your upkeep will be your downfall. Or, to put it another way: You definitely can make mistakes, but you can't make mistakes indefinitely.

What I'd suggest is getting in the habit of paying yourself first—that is, writing a check to your savings plan or mutual fund account *before* you start paying your bills. That'll force you to cut back elsewhere instead of making your future a low priority. Ten percent of your salary might be a good ultimate goal to shoot for when paying yourself. But you may have to work up to that. Remember: The average retiree depends on personal savings to provide nearly 18 percent of his or her retirement income.

Although it's true that money talks, the only thing it says to some people is "good-bye." If you're one of those people, then you really need to get in the savings habit.

Third, *live long*. A person who has saved $150,000 at age 60 will, at 7 percent interest, have $295,000 at age 70, $580,000 at 80, and $1.1 million when he or she is 90. Each extra decade does wonders for wealth, if not for health.

Thus, the surest way to make any portfolio grow faster is to get out of the spending habit, start saving more money earlier, and then keep on doing it.

2. Get Out of Debt, Especially Credit-Card Debt

When I give seminars, I often joke: "A thief stole my wife's credit cards. But I haven't turned him in yet. So far he's charging less than she did!" It gets a laugh, but it's a guilty laugh, closer to the truth than many listeners would wish.

In truth, needless debt is no laughing matter. Consumers rarely fall deeply into debt all at once. Instead, their expenses outpace their income little by little until the amount owed is overwhelming. Often, credit cards are at the root of that bad habit.

Buying more than you can afford to pay off at the end of the month is a double danger. One, it's likely to preclude you from saving any of your income. And two, such debt takes a huge chunk out of your future wealth.

Credit card charges—*surprise!*—are loans with very expensive interest charges. In fact, the average family owes more than $8,000 on credit cards alone. That's ridiculous! Doubly so since credit-card debt is no longer tax-deductible.

Credit cards are an excellent cash-management tool in disciplined hands—you can actually use the bank's money and defer payment for a month. Besides, plastic has become almost a necessity when traveling, and in an emergency, credit cards are wonderful. But put them in nondisciplined hands in a nonemergency, and the results can be disastrous.

About 70 percent of credit-card users don't pay in full each month. But paying 17 percent or 18 percent or more on your outstanding balance is a fool's game. (Not to mention often paying an annual fee on top of that.) That's at least 15 percent more than you're getting on your savings account. Does that make sense? Or put another way, wouldn't it make more sense to take those savings and pay off the card?

Look at it as an investment. If you pay off your 18 percent credit card, it's tantamount to *earning* 18 percent, guaranteed and tax-free. Not a bad move, right? Other suggestions:

- *Know your card.* Understand the terms. Many card issuers offer low introductory rates. Then after a few months, they raise the rate sharply on some or all of your purchases.
- *Cough up more than the minimum.* If you can't pay off the balance at month's end, try for some damage control by at least sending in more than the minimum payment. Paying only the monthly minimum on an $1,800 balance on an 18 percent credit card means that it'll take more than 13 years to eliminate that debt.
- *If all else fails.* If you absolutely can't find the discipline to pay off your card each month, consider canceling or cutting up your cards. Or failing that, switch to a charge card, like American Express, rather than a credit card; charge cards *must* be paid off each month. Or switch to a debit card, which pays

for your purchases by withdrawing money from your bank account at no additional cost to you.

3. Maximize Contributions to Your 401(k) or Pension Plan

Contributing to your employer-sponsored retirement plan—especially if the employer matches your contribution—is as close as you can get to free money. If you work for a private firm, that plan is probably a 401(k)—named for the tax code section that created it; at a nonprofit, it may be called a 403(b).

Use it to the fullest extent possible. Why? Because if you belong to a plan that allows you to invest pretax dollars and you are in, say, the 25 percent tax bracket, you in effect make an immediate 25 percent on your investment—before it even starts to grow! That's because you're not reporting as income the amount you are saving. It's tough to beat that!

In addition, all the earnings from that contribution are tax-deferred, meaning you don't pay taxes until you retire. Plus, many companies match your contribution, often 50 cents to your dollar. That's another 50 percent profit! Between taxes not paid, taxes deferred, and company matching, this is almost like robbery without a gun! Yet nearly one-third of workers who have access to a plan do *not* contribute to it. *Pul-eez!* Take advantage of it.

With such a plan, you usually get the choice of having your money in one or more of several vehicles. Commonly these include fixed-interest investments (such as CDs or money markets); bond mutual funds; a balanced mutual fund; diversified stock funds including index funds, small-cap funds, and a host of others; or shares of your employer's stock.

Because retirement is a long-term proposition, most investors should use their 401(k) plan as a Bucket No. 3 asset. However, those who will be in a low income tax bracket at retirement will want to begin moving some money into a Bucket No. 2 safety account a few years before they retire because it's sometimes better to draw down retirement funds if they can be spent in the lowest income tax bracket.

Also, a quick note on employer stock: It can make you rich or drive you to the poor house, depending on the your company's performance. Since even the best of companies have had periods in which their stock price dropped by 30 or 50 percent or more, it's wise to limit the amount of company stock in your 401(k) to no more than 25 percent of the total.

4. Investigate Your Pension Plan

A pension plan is one in which your employer promises to give you a specific monthly income for life, starting at retirement, or perhaps a lump sum. These are called *defined benefit plans*. The amount you get depends on your salary, age, number of years with that employer, and other factors.

Fewer than one-half of retirees receive income from a pension plan, a figure that's been declining because of the growth of the self-employed, temporary, and part-time workforce and because of the popularity of the 401(k). But if you're eligible for a pension, you need to learn the specifics.

Because the plan and its formula are different at every company, it's important to find out, for example, about the vesting schedule (how many years of service before you become partially or fully eligible), what happens if you quit your job, and what the pension plan is invested in and how financially sound is the plan. Also check on how much you can expect to receive, say, at age

60, 62, or 65. Find out what the benefits are for your survivor if you die and whether there is a cost-of-living adjustment.

When you do retire, you'll probably be offered a single-life annuity (a monthly income for life but which stops at your death) or a joint and survivor annuity (a smaller amount that continues as long as either you or your spouse is alive.) Most workers chose the latter. But *should* they?

In effect, by choosing the joint and survivor annuity, you're buying a life insurance policy for your surviving spouse. The cost of such a policy is the difference between the payout of the two benefit plans—usually several hundred dollars per month. If you already have sufficient life insurance to cover your survivor's needs, you may be better off taking the single-life annuity. Or, with part of the additional income you'll get by not taking the survivor benefit, you can buy your own insurance policy rather than having the company do it for you.

Doing so brings other advantages besides being possibly cheaper: You can get a lump sum from the insurance instead of a monthly check that a pension plan provides. And you can change the beneficiary as well as leave some of the proceeds to heirs, neither of which is possible with the pension plan.

Again, careful attention must be paid to any decision relating to pension distributions, lump sums, cost-of-living adjustments (COLAs), and the like. This is all the more reason to hire a good financial planner.

5. Do Something about Your Estate

"Estate" sounds so pretentious, like something only somebody like Bill Gates might have. But, in truth, everybody has one, even if it's just an undernourished bank account and a ratty, old car. Your estate is just what you own minus what you owe. And the purpose of estate planning is to answer the questions: Who gets what? And under what conditions?

Estate planning can help ensure that your money and other assets go to the people you want—not those determined by state law. Further, it allows you to divide your assets in such a way as to provide for efficient money management, create the fewest possible legal hassles for your survivors, and possibly minimize the tax bite.

To do this, you first want to figure out what your assets are and how much you want to pass on to heirs. Then come up with a plan that takes into account probate (the legal process that distributes your estate) and estate taxes, which are transfer taxes that can take a big chunk out of your estate if it's over a certain amount ($1.5 million, starting in 2004). That limit will be raised over the next few years, and then the estate tax is totally repealed in the year 2010. (In 2011 the law is destined to revert back to the rules in existence in 2001. Go figure!) To do even a halfway decent job of this, you're probably going to need the help of professionals, such as an estate-planning lawyer and a CERTIFIED FINANCIAL PLANNER™.

Some of the issues you may want to discuss include:

- *Writing a will.* Having a will streamlines the process. If you die without having written a will, the state government will provide a standard one according to its laws, and that may be something quite different than what you intended. Do you really want the state making decisions such as who will raise your kids and who will get your money? But you don't want just *any* will. You want one tailored for you with some thought, not just a fill-in-the-blanks standard form. Will-writing software programs are cheap, but spending a little bit on a lawyer is usually a much better idea. One of the biggest flaws of a one-size-fits-all will is that many times named heirs are able to receive assets without restrictions. But often restrictions are needed. For instance, do you want to be sure your 20-year-old spends his inheritance on college, not on a sports car? Are you confident your grandchild will be a good steward of his or her inheritance and will invest it wisely? Or should a bank or trust company watch over the assets until he or she is more capable? Do you want to be sure an ex-spouse doesn't walk away with assets you intended for your grandkids? All of this can be accomplished with properly drafted wills and trusts.

- *What stays out of the will?* All wills must be validated by a probate court. This takes time, can cost attorney's fees, and is a public (not a private) process. So most people prefer to avoid probate as much as possible. Ways to do that include titling many assets jointly and/or setting up a living trust (see below). When a person dies, some assets—such as joint accounts and those that name a beneficiary, like life insurance and IRAs—go immediately to the co-owner or to the named beneficiary. Everything else is passed to the heirs according to the will.

- *Setting up a living trust.* This is a popular way of seeing that other assets, such as your home, bank accounts, and brokerage accounts, are kept out of probate. A big advantage is that although you've placed assets in trust, you can name yourself as trustee and keep control over them until you die, when the assets then pass immediately to your beneficiaries. Among a living trust's many advantages are that it's nearly impossible to challenge and it's valid throughout the United States, unlike wills. Further, most people opt for a *revocable* living trust, meaning they can change or cancel the trust arrangement at any point during their lifetime. Even if you have a living trust, you probably should still have a will. A couple of important points: First, a trust is really just a container, an envelope of sorts. It has no intrinsic value and no worth until and unless you retitle assets into the trust. Otherwise, all that legal effort is fruitless. Second, it avoids probate but not taxes. Your heirs will get their legacy sooner than they otherwise would, but they still may need to pay taxes on it if the estate exceeds the tax-free limits.

■ *The role of multiple trusts.* A comprehensive estate plan may consist of several trusts. These can be set up for a number of different purposes. To cite just a few:

- ■ Generation-skipping trusts allow income from your trust to be used by your children, although some or all of the principal passes to your grandchildren.
- ■ Bypass trusts (also called *AB* or *Martial Life Estate* trusts) provide for your spouse upon your death. But then the trust assets pass tax-free to the trust's final beneficiaries (usually your kids) upon your spouse's death.
- ■ QTIP (Qualified Terminable Interest Property) trusts ensure your surviving spouse gets income but that the assets eventually go to your children, not to a new spouse of your former husband or wife.
- ■ Charitable remainder trusts permit you to contribute assets to a charity and get a tax deduction as well as an annuity from the income.

■ *Including a living will.* A living will, usually part of a living trust, declares your preference for medical treatment if you become seriously ill. It often is accompanied by a *durable power of attorney for health care,* which appoints an adult to have legal authority to make medical decisions for you if you become incapacitated. A living will has nothing to do with a regular will, which divides property.

- *Including a durable power of attorney for financial matters.* Similar to the durable power of attorney for health care, this one allows you to name someone to handle your money if you cannot. This can avoid prolonged, costly court proceedings if you become incapacitated.

- *Gifting.* Another way of avoiding taxes—or shifting taxes to someone in a lower tax bracket—is giving away some of your assets while you're still alive. Most gifts are by older people to their children and grandchildren with an eye to helping them buy a house or get an education. Each year, you can give up to $11,000 ($22,000 from a married couple) to each family member or heir without gift or estate taxes. (By contrast, if the money stays in your estate, the tax at death could be as much as 55 percent.) If you have the cash flow and plan far enough ahead, you can avoid much in estate taxes through this strategy.

As you can see, there are lots of possibilities. What's more, estate plans require periodic review and revision if they are to stay current and viable, especially if your marital status changes, you change your state of residence, or your health or income changes.

6. Pay off Your Mortgage—*Maybe!*

Owning the family home free and clear is a goal of the mortgage-burdened everywhere. They dream of not having to write that check every month, and that's a worthy objective. But is it the best possible solution for everyone?

Certainly it would feel great to be freed from your mortgage. But wouldn't it feel even better to have the mortgage taken care of but still get that important tax deduction? If you're able to save to send in extra payments in hopes of paying off your home loan early, maybe you could put some or all of that money to work in a smarter way—say, a Roth IRA. Withdrawals from a Roth (named for a U.S. senator from Delaware who sponsored the legislation) are tax-free, provided you leave the money in the account for at least five years after making the first contribution and you're over 59½. (A Roth IRA doesn't require you to begin making withdrawals by 70½ or to stop making contributions after that age as does the traditional IRA.)

With the money that you'd otherwise use to make extra loan payments, you could build up a Roth and get a tax-free nut with which to pay down the loan. Yes, you'd still need to write that check each month to the bank or savings and loan. But if you knew the tax-free source from which the money was coming— and you kept what's likely your biggest tax deduction—wouldn't it be worth it? Think about it.

7. Do Some Straight Thinking about Life Insurance

There's an awful lot of confusion about insurance in general. But here's the bedrock truth: *The aim of all insurance is to protect against the risk of financial loss.* The aim for most individuals isn't necessarily to make money from their insurance or to protect against emotional loss (which is impossible), but rather find the least expensive solution to the need for protection.

Folks rarely complain when they make it through another year without collecting on their life insurance. But they do complain that they don't understand insurance. Indeed, the mechanics and the nomenclature—*term, whole, universal, variable,* and the like—can be confusing.

What's even more confusing is some of the misinformation that is occasionally doled out by the financial press, talking heads, and sometimes even the insurance industry itself. My advice: Unless you are in a high tax bracket or have surplus cash to invest beyond your retirement plans and Roth IRA, buy life insurance not as an investment but for protection against financial loss—like dying and leaving your dependents without a breadwinner.

To cover such a loss, you should buy the cheapest form of term life insurance. However, for certain individuals it may actually be cheaper in the long run to buy a permanent policy, especially if they overfund it and build up a significant cash value. That way, in the later years when term insurance is very expensive, the permanent policy may have accumulated enough equity to cover the long-term cost of the mortality expense. Variable life policies allow the cash value to be invested in subaccounts like stock mutual funds, and the mortality expense is withdrawn tax-free from the earnings. It's like buying term insurance and investing the difference in a tax-sheltered environment.

As a general rule, those with limited cash flow and a high need for temporary coverage should buy term insurance. Those in high tax brackets who either can't qualify for Roth IRAs or are already funding them may want to consider permanent insurance like whole life, universal life, or variable universal life. In most cases a combination of the two—term and permanent—makes the most sense: term for your short-term needs and permanent for long-term needs and supplemental, tax-favored savings.

It's important to evaluate your particular situation before deciding which type or types of life insurance work best for you. This is yet another area in which a solid financial planner can help.

8. Know What Else You Need to Protect Against

As you approach your retirement years, ask yourself: What are my biggest potential financial losses? Well, your house could burn down, your job could disappear, or through injury or illness, you could become unable to take care of yourself.

You probably already have fire insurance, and you might be able to replace your job. But what if you lost your ability to produce an income? Or, if you're not working, what if you were forced to enter a nursing home? Either would qualify as a major financial reversal, the kind that insurance is best designed for. So you should also consider:

- *Disability insurance.* If you become sick or injured and can't work, that's when big trouble begins. You could lose your home, your ability to put your kids through school, and your shot at building a retirement nest egg. After all, medical advances can keep you alive in cases where you would have died a generation ago—but that doesn't mean you won't be devastated by the costs and by the loss of income.

    Disability insurance *is* expensive. But guess why: Because there's a good chance you're going to need to file a claim. In fact, insurers figure that you're five times more likely to be disabled than to die during your working life. Of course, if you weren't likely to need it, the policy would be cheap. But is that a reason not to have it? I don't think so.

    Be very careful when buying disability insurance. Do a lot of research and compare and contrast policies on such points as the definition of disability, the waiting period (known as the *elimination* period) after being disabled before you get the benefits, monthly income, cost-of-living adjustments, what kind or amount of work you may continue to do if you're able, and the *integration,* or how the policy meshes with other benefits or income you receive.

■ *Long-term care insurance.* Although disability insurance is important for the nonretired, the big issue for retirees becomes long-term care insurance (LTCI). LTCI is a question you could someday face for yourself, and maybe even sooner for your parents. Today's extended life spans have upped the odds of suffering heart attacks, cancer, strokes, or Alzheimer's disease. Even a broken hip or a bout of pneumonia can devour decades of savings in a matter of months if you need home health care or need to be admitted to a long-term care facility. So LTCI is a good way of avoiding a terrible cash drain in your retirement years.

More than half the women and about a third of men who reach age 65 will spend some time in a nursing home. And it ain't cheap, running in the $40,000-to-$60,000-a-year range —and neither private health insurance nor Medicare pays for it. So unless you're very wealthy, this should be a priority.

The cost of LTCI is directly related to your age, so there's an advantage in buying it early (because it'll be cheaper), but probably not too early (because you'll be paying premiums to guard against a very unlikely event). So late middle age, say, your fifties or early sixties, is probably the optimal time.

The policy should contain benefits that will pay for care wherever you'll likely to need it: at home, in adult day care, assisted living, or a nursing home. It also should include inflation protection. Your state insurance department sets the standards for this type of policy, and you might want to check with that agency, or with an advisor who specializes in LTCI, before you buy.

Once purchased, the cost of the policy usually remains the same for life. (Even wealthy folks often buy LTCI because, while they could afford long-term care, they'd rather spend a few hundred dollars a year on a policy than expend their assets on the care itself and thus, short-change their heirs.) LTCI is worth thinking about, especially when you're young enough to afford it and your health is good enough to qualify for it.

9. Level with Your (Adult) Kids

You owe it to your children—and to yourself—to be more forthcoming about money than your parents probably were with you. Just telling your kids, "everything is taken care of," isn't enough. After all, they may be forced to make vital health care choices without understanding what kind of insurance you have, to take care of your house and car without knowing the name of your insurance agent, and to pay bills without even being sure of where you keep the checkbook. What's more, if they are likely to inherit some money—or not inherit any—that's information that would be very helpful to them for planning purposes.

Poor parent-child communication can cause big money problems. A worst-case scenario: The parent could have a major stroke without having authorized a power of attorney. Thus, even the children do not have the legal authority to pay the parent's bills or file the parent's taxes. The children might even need to seek a court-appointed conservator, a difficult process that could run up huge legal fees.

Why is it so hard for the generations to talk? Discussing death and disability isn't a million laughs, and such a discussion reminds us of an unwanted change in the relationship. The parents feel old, and signing a power of attorney feels like losing control. Plus, many adult children don't feel competent themselves when it comes to money.

Nonetheless, such talks are absolutely necessary. Most people, if they get up the nerve at all, wait until parents are old and frail. But the best time to have a financial dialogue is when parents are, say, in their fifties or at the latest in their sixties.

You should make sure your kids know:

- Where you store your financial records, including tax returns, pension information, and investment data.
- What kind of medical insurance you have.
- Who your doctors are and what kind of medications you take.
- The status of your estate planning, including wills and trusts.
- Who is the executor of your will.
- How you would expect to handle the costs of an extended illness.
- Where your emergency paperwork is kept, including powers of attorney, will, living wills, and trusts.
- Your monthly income and expenses.
- How you plan to divide your assets.
- The names, addresses, and phone numbers of all your advisors, including estate lawyer, accountant, investment advisors, trust officers, insurance agent, banker, and the like.

10. Never Forget That Investing Is a Marathon, Not a Sprint

Even with all the market's dips and dives, the odds still favor investors who diversify and keep their money long term in stocks. Your *Buckets of Money* philosophy should be a powerful inducement to long-term thinking.

I know I've said this before. In fact, it's a theme of this book, but it bears repeating: To be successful in your retirement planning, you've got to think long term. The average Wall Street investor is a sprinter who looks for the best possible short-term return. But you're a marathoner. You seek long-term results. This philosophy may give you short-run pain from time to time but, with any kind of luck, it will give you long-run joy.

Your goal is to build a winning, long-term portfolio. To do so, try to:

- *Stay firmly focused on the future.* Remind yourself not to be too concerned about whether the market is up or down today, whether the Fed will or will not lower or raise interest rates, or whether Wall Street likes or hates the newest crop of presidential contenders. Instead, ask yourself if the long-term prospects for the U.S. economy are solid and whether the long-term prospects for American business and industry are good. Know that good times are always alloyed with bad, that in the last half century there have been 14 bear markets (occurring roughly every 3.5 years), and, further, that four wars, nine recessions, eight presidents, and one impeachment since World War II didn't keep profits from going up 55-fold and the stock market up 60 times.

- *Avoid panic.* Obsessively watching CNBC or CNNfn can leave you with the impression of an impending Armageddon or lead you to believe you can get rich quick. But the truth is that compulsively watching even the best financial networks or reading even the top financial newspapers or magazines can be a little bit like trying to tell the time by looking only at the second hand of your watch. Instead, be a long-term investor who makes rational, informed decisions and accepts a certain amount of volatility as a fact of financial life. People who think logically are a nice contrast to the rest of the world, and as a result, they likely will prosper.

- *Be committed to investing in equities.* Lack of patience is probably the single, biggest obstacle to successful stock market investing. When there's a downturn, don't think about how much you've lost—think about how many more shares you can now purchase for the same amount of money. Successful long-term investors see downturns, painful as they are, as buying opportunities.

- *Guard against overconfidence.* The ancient law of investing— Be fearful when others are greedy and greedy when others are fearful—is still in effect. Excessive hubris is one of the biggest threats to any investor. Remember, you don't need market-beating returns to do well. Just matching, or nearly matching, the market over a period of time will probably be just fine.

- *Keep diversified.* Hot stocks, hot sectors, and hot styles of investing come and go like summer squalls. The successful, long-term investor is the one who invests broadly, rebalances, and stays invested in both bearish and bullish periods.

- *Get right with risk.* Extra risk may lead to extra returns—but it's not guaranteed. On the other hand, to get extra returns, you *do* have to take extra risk. So develop a comfort level that works for you, and stick to it.

- *Know that the long-term trend is your friend.* The Baby Boomers—that huge demographic wave that's entering middle age—need the stock market for funding both their retirement and their children's education. So it's very likely they will continue to pour available savings into stocks. By and large, these are savvy, long-term players who are better informed than investors in the past and more likely to remain calmer during downturns. In addition, Boomers will receive over $10 trillion from their parents in the next 15 to 20 years. Where else will that go long term but into equities, the stock market, and real estate?

So, if you want a comfortable retirement, you've got to be willing to take some risks with equity investments, spend less, save more, and continue to educate yourself in the ins and outs of modern financial planning. This isn't, as the saying goes, rocket science. But it does take some thought and some effort. Or as someone once noted: Success is a matter of luck—just ask any failure.

Whew! That's it. That's all the advice I can muster for now. After all, I'm not young enough to know everything. But I have told you a great deal that I've learned in almost three decades of being a financial advisor. Except for one overarching and not inconsequential suggestion in the next chapter.

CHAPTER 14

Enjoying Life As a *Bucketeer*

"Money is better than poverty, if only for financial reasons," Woody Allen once said, and he's right. All things being equal, it's better to be rich than poor. But as we know, all things aren't equal, and I want to end this book with what I hope is a bit of perspective.

For many pages now I've talked about how to make your retirement financially secure. Obviously, that's important *up to a point.* But if you get too far beyond that point, if you get to where the digits, decimal points, and dollar signs obscure life's other joys, you've gone too far.

Making money for people, managing people's money is my calling, my livelihood, and my passion. There's nothing I'd rather be doing as an occupation. But I'd be lying if I told you it was the most important thing in the world for me as I roll out of bed in the morning. For me, that most important thing is family. My wife Jeanne and our kids and my extended family are at the center of my solar system. Money is just how I earn my living and keep those planets spinning.

I sometimes reflect on the words of Charlie Munger, Warren Buffet's sidekick: "If all you succeed in doing in life is getting rich by buying little pieces of paper, it's a failed life," he said. "Life is more than being shrewd in wealth accumulation." I couldn't agree more.

The Variety of Riches

Money is a two-edged sword. It's been called the root of all evil. And that's probably true. But it's a fact that money is the root of a lot of other things, too. And, by golly, we need roots. So, yes, you need money to retire and I hope *Buckets of Money* will make that possible in abundance. But you also need engagement and connection with people and pursuits. If you're never rich in anything but friends, family, and worthwhile things to do, you're still pretty rich.

We all recognize that some people get more joy out of life than others do. The same is true in retirement. This joy doesn't correlate with how much money you have. It correlates, I believe, with how *involved* you are. Involved with your family, friends, country, and planet. Involved with trying to make life better for others. Involved with physical activity and mental stimulation. Involved with romantic love. Involved with pets and grandchildren and the PTA, woodworking and model-airplane flying, guitar picking, raising roses, or anything else that interests you.

Interest is the key. And I don't just mean simple or compound interest. I mean your degree of interest in the world around you. There's no substitute for that.

What's Money Mean to You?

You probably won't have as much money in retirement as you did when working. Thus, it's important to understand what money means to you—to sort out your fiscal priorities, to break what's probably a family code of silence about money, and to come to grips with your money attitudes. That can be a chore but a liberation, too.

Does your attitude toward money help you lead an emotionally healthy life or does it represent an obstacle to achieving that? Do you rule money or does money rule you? Ruling money means knowing what your priorities are, knowing what you're ready to give up, and knowing what are acceptable trade-offs.

Much of this book has been aimed at trying to help you stave off fears about retirement, fears that you won't have enough money. I hope I've helped you allay those concerns. But I also want to make the point that money should represent freedom and an expanded lust for life, not just security. Being successful in the retirement game doesn't mean becoming the richest guy in the cemetery. It means living as richly as possible during the latter third or so of your life.

A lot of us give lip service to the idea that accumulating money now will allow us later to do what we really want to do. And that's true. But not if we keep postponing forever what it is we really want to do. Living well doesn't always depend on having more money or more things.

Here's the ultimate question: *What do you want to do with the rest of your life?* Start a business? Write a novel? Visit each of the national parks? Work for charities? Help save the environment? Or just play lots of golf?

What's your personal vision of how the world could be improved? What causes could you serve, injustices could you correct or dreams could you fulfill? And how are you situated to reach those goals? What are your unique needs and talents? What more do you need to learn and how do you need to grow before you can have a realistic shot at attaining your objectives? How can you best contribute to others? What have you learned in life that's worth passing along?

I urge you to take the time to think about questions like these and act upon the answers. I believe you'll find out you're surrounded by opportunities. Even if you're not going to retire with a small fortune, there is much to be done for yourself and others.

No Safety in Numbers

Our culture has come to accept great wealth as a personal value. But, in my view, life is so short, and there is no safety in numbers or anything else. So my advice would be: Don't let your wealth, or your pursuit of wealth, blind you or shield you from life.

Sure, save. Invest. Use your head to make your money go as far as you can. But don't let money, or lack of it, keep you from jumping on life's carousel. In short, living well doesn't always depend on having more money. Needs and expenses have an amazing ability to keep pace with income. So you can decide to make more, or you can decide to need less.

Whatever you decide, try to see your money as a tool of liberation, not a financial ball and chain. A common mistake many people make is not paying enough attention to their finances. But you also can pay *too much* attention. We regret more things we didn't do than those we did. And as others have said, the best things in life aren't things.

For a final word on the subject, I defer to Henrik Ibsen, the playwright, who wrote: "Money may be the husk of many things, but not the kernel. It brings you food, but not appetite; medicine but not health; acquaintances, but not friends; servants, but not faithfulness; days of joy, but not peace or happiness."

Go forth, enjoy, and prosper!

APPENDIX A

Recommended Books

Jonathan Clements, *25 Myths to Avoid—If You Want to Manage Your Money Right: The New Rules for Financial Success* (Fireside/Simon & Schuster, 1998).

Harry S. Dent, Jr., *The Great Boom Ahead: Your Comprehensive Guide to Personal and Business Profit in the New Era of Prosperity* (Hyperion, 1993).

____, *The Roaring 2000s: Building the Wealth and Lifestyle You Desire in the Greatest Boom in History* (Simon & Schuster, 1998).

Nancy Dunnan, *Dun & Bradstreet Guide to Your Investments, 1999* (HarperPerennial, 1999).

Ric Edelman, *The New Rules of Money* (HarperCollins, 1998).

____, *The Truth about Money,* 2nd ed. (HarperBusiness, 1998).

Jordan Goodman, *Dictionary of Finance and Investment Terms,* 5th ed. (Barrons Educational Series, 1998).

____, *Everyone's Money Book,* 3rd ed. (Dearborn Trade, 2001).

Gary L. Klott, *The New York Times Complete Guide to Personal Investing* (Times Books, 1987).

Lynn O'Shaughnessy, *The Retirement Bible* (Hungry Minds, 2001).

Barbara Stanny, *Prince Charming Isn't Coming: How Women Get Smart about Money* (Viking, 1997).

Larry E. Swedroe, *Rational Investing in Irrational Times: How to Avoid the Costly Mistakes Even Smart People Make Today* (St. Martin's Press, 2002).

Ralph Warner, *Get a Life: You Don't Need a Million to Retire Well* (Nolo, 1996).

Helpful Online Sites

Here are just a few of the hundreds, if not thousands, of helpful web sites. Many of these allow you to track your investments as well as learn about personal finance and follow financial news.

www.raylucia.com
My web site offers various educational materials to assist with your *Buckets* planning, including worksheets, calculators, a database of financial articles, an online stream of my nationally syndicated radio show, and my seminar schedule.

www.collegeparents.org
This private membership organization is aimed at helping parents cope with college expenses.

www.marketwatch.com
This site, similar to ABC's, is operated by the CBS network.

www.money.com
The site, run by CNN and *Money* magazine, includes general financial and budgeting information as well as several calculators for help in making financial decisions.

http://moneycentral.msn.com
This one, run by Microsoft, also includes news and personal finance information as well as a search mechanism for finding financial planners.

www.moneyzone.com

Oriented more toward entrepreneurs, this site includes businesses for sale as well as funding opportunities.

www.morningstar.com

This is the definitive site for mutual fund information.

www.napfa.org and **www.fpanet.org**

These professional organizations provide search mechanisms to allow you to find financial planners who practice near you.

www.sec.gov and **www.nasd.com**

These governmental or quasi-governmental agencies keep records on brokers, planners, and other financial professionals.

Glossary

401(k).   An employer-sponsored retirement plan in which employees can contribute pretax dollars, and the money grows tax-deferred until it is withdrawn. Named after a section of the federal tax code.

403(b).   An employer-sponsored retirement plan for employees of tax-exempt organizations, such as schools, charities, and hospitals. Workers can contribute pretax dollars, and the money grows tax-deferred until it is withdrawn. Named for a section of the federal tax code.

A

Aggressive growth fund.   A mutual fund that normally invests in small or fast-growing firms.

Analyst.   An expert employed by an investment house, brokerage, or mutual fund who analyzes corporations and makes recommendations about whether the securities issued by that corporation should be bought or sold. Typically, analysts specialize in a particular industry, such as energy or pharmaceuticals.

Annuity.   Usually, an insurance product purchased to provide monthly payments during retirement.

Asset allocation.   The process of deciding how to divide a portfolio among stocks, bonds, and cash.

Asset class.   A group of assets—such as cash, real estate, or equities —with similar risk and reward characteristics.

B

Balanced fund. A mutual fund that seeks to provide current income as well as growth with a portfolio of stocks, bonds, and cash.

Bear market. A prolonged decline in the stock market.

Benchmark. An appropriate standard against which actively managed funds can be judged. For example, the performance of small-cap managers should be compared to a small-cap index such as the Russell 2000.

Blue-chip stock. The stock of a well-known corporation with a long record of growth.

Bond. An instrument of debt issued by corporations and governments. The issuer commits to regular interest payments to the lenders (bondholders) and ultimately repays the original investment in a specified number of years. If a firm is liquidated, bondholders are given a higher priority than stockholders and thus have a better chance of getting some of their money back.

Bond ladder. An investment strategy in which a portfolio is structured so as to have roughly equal amounts invested in various maturities. Thus, interest payments come due sequentially.

Broker. A person who charges a fee or commission for trading stocks, bonds, and other securities.

Bull market. A market in which prices of securities are generally rising. A person who expects prices will move higher is called a *bull,* and an event is considered *bullish* when it's expected to move prices higher.

Buy and hold. A long-term strategy to purchase stocks or mutual funds and keep them despite the ups and downs of the stock market.

C

Capital appreciation. The increase in the market value of an asset since it was purchased.

Capital gain. The net profit made when assets such as stocks, bonds, and real estate are sold for more than the original purchase price.

Capital gains distribution. A payment by a mutual fund to its shareholders for the profits made on the sale of stocks or bonds in the fund's portfolio. Shareholders are liable for taxes on these gains even though they did not sell their mutual fund shares.

Capital gains taxes. The taxes on profits from the sale of securities or real estate.

Capitalization. The market value of a company as determined by multiplying the number of outstanding shares times the price per share of its stock.

Certificate of deposit (CD). An interest-bearing deposit at a bank that locks up an investor's money for a certain period of time, such as six months or a year. CDs normally pay a higher interest rate than savings accounts.

CERTIFIED FINANCIAL PLANNER™ (CFP®). A financial advisor who has passed a rigorous exam to certify his or her wide knowledge on a range of personal finance issues.

Certified Public Accountant (CPA). A person who has passed a rigorous exam to certify his or her knowledge of accounting, auditing, and tax issues.

Churning. Excessive trading by unethical brokers to generate more commissions from their clients.

Closed-end funds. A type of mutual fund with a finite number of shares. Those shares are traded on the stock exchanges. In contrast to a traditional open-ended fund, the price investors are willing to pay isn't necessarily the same as the value of the fund's underlying holdings, or net asset value (NAV).

Commission. The fee paid to a broker for completing a trade.

Common stock. A class of securities representing ownership in a company. A holder of one or more shares is a part owner of the firm and thus is entitled to vote on company directors and receive dividends.

Compounding. Growth that results from reinvested income as well as from the gains on the original investment.

Consumer Price Index (CPI).   An index, calculated by the federal government, that seeks to measure the cost of buying a certain assortment of consumer goods. Cost-of-living increases to Social Security are linked to changes in the CPI.

Corporate bond.   A taxable bond issued by a corporation.

Cost basis.   The original cost of an investment that's used to specify the capital gain when the investment is sold.

D

Defined benefit plan.   A pension plan that guarantees a certain benefit based on a formula that includes salary history and years of service.

Defined contribution plan.   An employer-sponsored retirement plan that depends on employee contributions and often some employer contributions as well. The benefits, not guaranteed, depend on the success of the underlying investments.

Diversification.   Holding different types of investments to reduce risk.

Dividend.   A company's distribution of earnings to investors who own stock or who own shares in a mutual fund holding the stock of that firm.

Dividend reinvestment plan (DRIP).   A program through which investors, without using a broker, automatically reinvest dividends generated by stocks they own. Also known as a *direct reinvestment plan*.

Dollar-cost averaging.   Investing a set amount of money periodically, usually monthly or quarterly. The investor thus attempts to reduce the risk that might be involved in investing a large sum all at once.

Dow Jones Industrial Average (DJIA).   The nation's most closely watched stock market index, it consists of a weighted average of the stock of 30 major corporations.

E

EE bonds.   A traditional type of government bond in which the bond is purchased at half its face value; then the interest gradually builds up until the bond is worth its face value.

Emerging market fund. A mutual fund that invests in stocks of firms located in less developed countries.

Estate tax. A federal tax levied on some large estates when the owner dies.

Exchange traded fund (ETF). A basket of securities designed to track an index while still trading as a stock.

Expense ratio. A charge that investors pay annually to a mutual fund. It's expressed as a percentage of the total investment and may include management, administrative, and marketing fees.

F

Federal Deposit Insurance Corp (FDIC). A federal agency that guarantees a customer's money (up to a certain limit) will be protected if the bank fails.

Federal Reserve Bank. The central bank that sets U.S. monetary policy. The "Fed," along with its Federal Open Market Committee, oversees the money supply, interest rates, and credit.

Fee-based planner. A financial advisor who is paid through a combination of fees and commissions.

Fee-only planner. A financial advisor who is not paid by commission. Some are paid by the hour or by the project, while others charge a percentage of assets.

Financial advisor. A generic term used by many money consultants, such as financial planners, brokers, and insurance agents.

Fixed annuity or GIC (Guaranteed Investment Contract). A contractual arrangement in which an investor, in return for a lump sum, receives a set sum of money at regular intervals for a specific period of time or for life. It's similar to a tax-deferred CD but is offered by an insurance company.

Front-end load. An up-front sales commission paid when shares of certain mutual funds are purchased.

G

Growth and income fund. A mutual fund that invests in corporations that are expected both to grow and produce dividends.

Growth fund.   A mutual fund that invests in firms that are expected to grow rapidly and thus produce significant returns.

Growth stock.   A stock that sells for a high price relative to its earnings.

I

I Bond.   A government bond that provides both a fixed rate of return as well as an inflation-protection component.

Immediate annuity or IAC (Immediate Annuity Contract).   A contractual arrangement with an insurance company in which an investor, in return for a lump sum, receives a set sum of money at regular intervals for a specific period of time or for life.

Index.   A composite of securities that measures price changes in a specific group.

Index fund.   A mutual fund that seeks to match the returns of a stock or bond benchmark by holding the same stocks or bonds that comprise the index.

Individual Retirement Account (IRA).   A savings vehicle in which investors are allowed to deposit money to grow tax-deferred until taken out in retirement. *See also Roth IRA.*

Inflation.   A time of generally rising consumer prices, generally expressed as a percentage of increase above the previous year's prices.

J

Joint-and-survivorship pension.   A pension covering a worker and his or her spouse and paying benefits until both have died.

Junk bonds.   High-yield corporate bonds that are rated below investment grade. While the riskiest of all bonds, these are also potentially the highest-yielding.

L

Large-cap stocks.   Stocks of the largest corporations, whose capitalization (share price times number of shares outstanding) exceeds $10 billion.

Leading indicators. Major market signs that suggest the economic state for the coming months. Indicators include consumer expectations, changes in the money supply, and price fluctuations.

Leverage. The use of debt to increase the amount of assets that can be acquired.

Liquidity. The ability to quickly sell to produce cash.

Load. A mutual fund sales charge used to pay a stockbroker's or financial advisor's commission.

Long-term care insurance. A policy that pays for nursing home and/or home care expenses when the policyholder can no longer take care of himself or herself.

M

Margin. Buying securities on credit.

Market capitalization. The market price per share times the number of shares.

Market timing. A strategy used by investors who seek to anticipate trends, that is, buying before a predicted upswing and selling when they expect a downturn.

Money market fund. A type of mutual fund that invests in short-term securities and usually keeps the per share value at $1.

Mortgage-backed securities. A financial instrument representing an interest in assets that are mortgage-related.

Municipal bonds. Obligations issued by state and local governments. Interest paid is free from federal income tax and in some cases free of state and local taxes as well.

Mutual fund. A pool of money from many shareholders that is invested in stocks or bonds and thus allows investors to own a small piece of many securities by holding shares of the fund.

N

NASDAQ 100. An index of the biggest and most popularly traded companies on the NASDAQ.

National Association of Securities Dealers (NASD). Virtually every securities firm doing business with the American public—including 5,300 brokerage firms and more than 664,000 registered securities representatives—comes under its jurisdiction. This private, not-for-profit organization operates the NASDAQ, sets ethical guidelines for the industry, and investigates violations of its rules.

National Association of Securities Dealers Automated Quotation (NASDAQ). A computerized marketplace that handles trades for thousands of stocks, including those of many technology companies.

Net asset value (NAV). The value of a single share of a mutual fund's investments.

Net income. A firm's profits after taxes, depreciation, interest, and other expenses.

No-load fund. A mutual fund that does not impose a sales charge.

P

Pension plan. A fund established by a company for paying retirement benefits to former employees.

Portfolio. All securities held by an investor.

Preferred stock. A hybrid equity that functions a lot like a bond, paying income and giving investors a higher priority than common stockholders if the firm is liquidated.

R

Rally. A rise in stock or bond prices following a downward movement.

Real estate investment trust (REIT). A publicly owned company that acquires, owns, and manages income-producing real estate.

Rebalancing. Restoring a portfolio to its original asset allocation.

Recession. A downturn in economic activity, generally defined as two consecutive quarters of decline in a nation's gross domestic product.

Required minimum distribution (RMD). The amount of money that federal law requires to be withdrawn from a retirement account after the investor reaches age 70½.

Roth IRA. A savings vehicle in which investors are allowed to deposit money to grow tax-deferred and to withdraw it tax-free in retirement.

Russell 2000. The best-known small-cap stock index.

S

Sales load. A sales charge levied by some mutual funds.

Section 529 plans. State-sponsored college savings plans that allow investors to shelter from taxes the money they save for their children's education.

Securities. Common stocks, preferred stocks, corporate bonds, and government bonds.

Securities and Exchange Commission (SEC). A federal agency, created in 1934, that regulates the securities industry.

Series EE savings bonds. Savings bonds issued by the federal government that are redeemed for face value at maturity.

Share price. The price of a single share of stock.

Simple interest. Interest calculated on the original amount of money invested.

Simplified Employee Pensions-Individual Retirement Account (SEP-IRA). A retirement plan that allows the self-employed to save tax-deferred.

Short-term capital gains tax. The tax on the profit from an investment that is sold after being held for one year or less.

Small-cap stock. Stocks of relatively small corporations whose capitalization (share price times number of shares outstanding) is $2 billion or less.

Socially responsible fund. A mutual fund that invests only in firms considered to be socially conscious.

Speculator.   A securities trader who seeks to capitalize on short-term price movements.

Standard & Poor's 500 Index (S&P 500).   An index of the stocks of 500 large U.S. corporations.

Standard deviation.   A measure of volatility, or risk.

Stock.   A share of ownership in a corporation. Owning a share entitles one to be involved in a firm's growth or decline, receive dividends, choose directors, and to participate in other corporate actions.

Stock split.   A transaction in which a firm increases or decreases the number of outstanding shares and alters the price and dividend accordingly.

Style drift.   A departure from the original asset allocation of a portfolio, either by not rebalancing or by actively purchasing securities outside a particular asset class.

T

Tax-deferred.   Earnings remain untaxed until withdrawn.

Tax-free bonds (municipal bonds).   Bonds whose interest is paid free from federal income tax and in some cases free of state and local taxes as well.

Tax-managed mutual funds.   A fund that seeks to keep low the yearly tax burden of its investors.

Term life insurance.   Insurance that provides no investment value but yields a cash benefit to survivors when a policyholder dies.

Total return.   An investment's income as well as any capital appreciation.

Treasuries.   Any government securities offered by the U.S. Treasury.

Treasury bill (T-bill).   A short-term obligation of the federal government, maturing in 13 or 26 weeks.

Treasury bond.   A federal government obligation that matures in 10 years or more after issuance.

Treasury Inflation-Protected Securities (TIPS).   Government bonds that increase in value during inflationary times. The value of the TIPS principal is adjusted twice a year to reflect changes in the federal Consumer Price Index.

Treasury note. A federal government obligation that matures from 2 to 10 years after issuance.

Turnover. The percentage of the stocks in a mutual fund's portfolio that are sold each year.

U

Universal life insurance. A cash-value life insurance policy that provides a death benefit as well as an investment component.

V

Value stock. Stocks that sell for a low price relative to their earnings.

Variable annuity. An investment product that is part insurance policy, part mutual fund and whose return is *variable,* depending on how the mutual fund portion performs.

Variable life insurance or **Variable Universal Life (VUL).** A policy providing a death benefit but also serving as a tax-deferred investment vehicle. The rate of return on the investment portion is determined by the performance of the underlying securities.

Vesting. The right of an employee to receive a company retirement benefit if he or she has worked at the firm for a specified period of time.

Volatility. The tendency for price fluctuations over a period of time.

W

Whole life insurance. A policy providing a death benefit but also serving as a tax-deferred investment vehicle. Part of the premium pays for the death benefit and the rest is invested for the policyholder.

Y

Yield. Income received from an investment expressed as a percentage of the market price.

Z

Zero-coupon bond. A bond sold at a discount to its face value.

About the Author

Raymond J. Lucia, CFP®, a financial planner since 1974, manages more than $750 million in client assets. His nationally syndicated talk show, "The Ray Lucia Show," reaches hundreds of thousands of listeners daily and continues to grow in popularity. He lives in San Diego, California, where he heads the Raymond J. Lucia Companies, Inc.

A nationally renowned expert in the field of financial and business management, Ray was named by *Radio and Records* magazine as one of its "Rising Stars of 2001" for his entertaining and informative radio shows. His show has been described as a clinic on personal finance that covers a wide range of issues and provides a forum for listeners everywhere.

Dale Fetherling has written or co-authored a dozen nonfiction books and taught writing and editing at five colleges and universities. He's based in San Diego.

Index